THE OPPORTUNITY
IS AT HAND

Oneida County, New York
Colored Soldiers
in the Civil War

The Opportunity Is At Hand

Oneida County, New York
Colored Soldiers
in the Civil War

By Donald M. Wisnoski

SCHROEDER PUBLICATIONS
2003

Front Cover: Unidentified corporal serving in Company H of an unidentified infantry regiment. This wartime photograph was reproduced in the 1880's in Turner Falls, Massachusetts. This soldier probably served in either the 54th or 55th Massachusetts Volunteer Infantry. Four Oneida County colored men served in these two regiments. *(Author's Collection)*

Back Cover: This handsome, unidentified soldier represents the appearance of over 178,000 colored soldiers who fought in the Civil War. This soldier from Penn Yan, New York, sports the greatcoat with cape. His uniform has the look of being newly issued. Over 4,100 black soldiers from New York State served during the war. *(Author's Collection)*

Cover Design: Maria A. Dorsett Schroeder

Published by
SCHROEDER PUBLICATION:
131 Tanglewood Drive
Lynchburg, VA 24502
www.civilwar-books.com
civilwarbooks@yahoo.com

Printed by
Sheridan Books
Fredericksburg, Virginia

ISBN-1-889246-20-4

Dedicated to the memory

of my parents

Leo and Mary Wisnoski

TABLE OF CONTENTS

PHOTOGRAPHS

ACKNOWLEDGEMENTS

This book was completed through the support and aid of many fine and knowledgeable people. Without the expertise in photography of Richard Aust, Curator, the usage of several unusual Utica Street scenes would not have been possible. Katherine Dhalle shared freely of her information whenever approached about black soldiers in the Civil War era. Having the lack of computer skills, Kristen and Bob White, have unselfishly used their time and computers for my benefit for this project. A book is never written by one person without the guidance of others. Maria and Patrick Schroeder have given their talents in publishing and history to spur this piece of literature along successfully. Family support is one of the best feelings a person can have with a project like this. I respect the patience of my daughters, Holly and Samantha, my sister, Lee, and the constant prodding along of my brother Daniel and his wife Candace.

Individuals: Richard Aust, Curator, Oneida County Historical Society; Barbara Brooks, Director, Utica Public Library; Jan DeAmicus, Professor, Utica College; Katherine Dhalle, Rome, New York; Tony Fidd, Warrensburg, New York; John Gunderson, Lake George, New York; Rodger Haley, Utica, New York; Kevin Kelly, Rome Historical Society; JoAnne Kujawski, Oneida County Historical Society; Robert Lalli, Utica Public Library; Kevin Marken & Staff, Administrator, Oneida County Historical Society; Darby O'Brien, Director, Utica Public Library; Maria Schroeder, Editor & Chief, Schroeder Publications, Lynchburg, Virginia; Patrick Schroeder, Historian, Appomattox Court House National Historical Park, Appomattox, Virginia; Merry Speicher, Administrator, Rome Historical Society; Robert Sudakow, Focus Photo, New Hartford, New York; Robert Tegart, Clinton Historical Society; Robert and Kristen White, Fancy Gap, Virginia; Richard Williams, Clinton Historical Society; Daniel and Candace Wisnoski, Utica, New York.

Institutions: Clinton Historical Society, Clinton, New York; Oneida County Historical Society, Utica, New York; Rome Historical Society, Rome, New York; United States Military History Institute, Carlisle, Pennsylvania; Utica Public Library, Utica, New York; National Archives, Washington, DC.

Without the help of the above family and friends, this book would be in a state of limbo, my extended thanks to all.

Donald M. Wisnoski

FOREWORD

The Opportunity is at Hand aptly describes the research that was done for this book by Mr. Wisnoski over the last dozen years. There have been studies of United States Colored Troops focusing on famous units such at the 54th and 55th Massachusetts and the 14th Rhode Island Heavy Artillery, and on the contributions of Black soldiers as a whole. Yet, a concentrated study of colored soldiers from one geographical area, of men who served in various units, has not been delved into until now. Mr. Wisnoski has researched over 60 colored service men and women from Oneida County, New York, who served in twenty different units and organizations. Many were in the ranks of the 26th and 31st United States Colored Troops, although there was a smattering who served with the renowned 54th Massachusetts Infantry, the 14th Rhode Island Heavy Artillery, and various other units, as well as several veterans of the U. S. Navy. Mr. Wisnoski has assembled a good sampling of photos for the project—thirty related images and illustrations for this book, many which are published here for the first time.

Without Mr. Wisnoski's resurrecting the untold stories of these stalwart servicemen, soldiers, and sailors, they would certainly have remained in obscurity. The book reveals the eagerness of colored citizens to take part in the great struggle. The earliest man to enlist was John E. Lippins who joined the Navy on November 4, 1861. Several men served with the 16th New York Heavy Artillery as cooks until transferring to the United States Colored Regiments. A colored washerwoman went into the field with the 2nd New York Heavy Artillery. There were the three Pell brothers who served, as well as James and William Sutphen—a father and son in the 31st United States Colored Troops. There was William "Uncle Bill" Smith of the 14th Rhode Island Heavy Artillery (later the 11th United States Colored Heavy Artillery) who lived to be 113 years old. There was William Henry who weighed 397 pounds, and was turned down by the army because of his bulk. Unwilling to be denied his right to serve, Henry joined the navy and was stationed aboard the *Hornet*. There was Arlington Denike, who served on the *U. S. S. Vermont* and the *Preston*, and attained the rank of 1st class petty officer during his service. Then there were less stellar men like John

Green, of the 1st and 40th United States Colored Troops. Though wounded in battle in 1863, Green was later characterized as "utterly worthless as a soldier and a confirmed malingerer." Then there are a few of which little information could be attained, and we may never know more of these brave men.

Though most black men from Oneida County were born free, there were those such as Eli Baylis, an escaped slave, who served in the 1st Mississippi Cavalry (later known as the 3rd United States Colored Cavalry), and Robert "Uncle Bob" Wilson who was liberated from servitude from a plantation near Culpeper, Virginia, and who attached himself as a 'contraband' to Major Rufus Daggett of the 117th New York Infantry. Milton Frank was drafted in the summer of 1863, served bravely, and was twice wounded—the first time at the Battle of Olustee in Florida, then at Chaffin's Farm in Virginia, a wound that proved mortal. One highlight of the book is a half-dozen letters written by William Labiel of the 14th Rhode Island Heavy Artillery. Sadly, Labiel did not survive the war.

Mr. Wisnoski has also included three appendices. One lists the known burial sites for the African-American soldiers from Oneida County, another lists the 24 white United States Colored Troops officers who came from the county, and the last is General Daniel Butterfield's analysis of the use of black soldiers entitled "Memoranda With Regard to Colored Troops." Of the African-American men to serve from the county, five of these men died while in service, and another four were wounded. Nearly all suffered ill effects from harsh service. This book is a fitting tribute to men and women that left friends and family to perform their duty when their opportunity was at hand.

Patrick A. Schroeder
Lynchburg, Virginia

PREFACE

The subject of this narrative (colored soldiers in the Civil War) was brought to light by the chance discovery of Private Cornelius Harding's grave. A casual stroll through New Forest Hill Cemetery, in Utica, New York, revealed not one, but three black soldiers' burial sites. An old saying "Curiosity Killed the Cat" went into full mode. Years of research revealed over sixty black soldiers from Oneida County that fought in the Civil War. This number included some black veterans who had moved to the county for various reasons after the war.

When the war broke upon the nation in 1861, Oneida County had a black population of approximately 600 people. The male populace tendered their services when the appropriate time arrived. These sons of Africa proved their worth in the restoration of the Union and helped in securing their own rights as fellow American citizens.

This study hopes to educate future generations that the black men of Oneida County played an important role in the Civil War. Brief biographies will enlighten the reader that these men were real people. They walked in the same areas as we do now and saw the same sky and sun as we of the 21st Century. Nothing would probably ever have been recorded about these men if not for their military service.

After the war, many of the black Oneidians returned home. Some moved on to work elsewhere while others remained to become valued citizens of the region. Burial locations have been noted when possible.

Hopefully the reader will learn some small facts about these extraordinary United States Colored Troops and appreciate their service. A Sunday trip to the various cemeteries mentioned may bring the reader to truly understand that these men where once real flesh and blood. They sacrificed as much as their white counterparts to save the Union. Perhaps we would be living a different lifestyle if not for these unknown soldiers.

Donald M. Wisnoski
Chadwicks, New York

29TH CONNECTICUT VOLUNTEER INFANTRY

Private William Avery
29th Connecticut Volunteers
Age: 41
Height: 5'4 ½"
Birthplace: Connecticut
Occupation: Laborer

Avery enrolled as a private in Rome, New York, at the end of 1863. On January 6, 1864, he was mustered in at Bridgeport, Connecticut, to become a member of the 29th Connecticut Volunteers (Colored). At the time of his enlistment, Avery was married with two children and lived in Rome.

In the beginning of April 1864, the regiment was ordered to South Carolina, and in August of the same year, to Virginia. Avery was present during his regiment's campaigns outside Petersburg and Richmond. Altogether the 29th fought in nine major battles and numerous skirmishes. After the fall of Richmond, Avery and his unit were sent to Texas where he was honorably mustered out on October 24, 1865.

Avery returned to his family in Rome after the war and resumed his normal life. As with other veterans, he was plagued by wartime illnesses until his death on June 5, 1884. His wife, Christy, had the help of another colored veteran, George Hall, of Rome, in trying to secure a pension. It is not known if she ever received a pension. Her husband was buried in Section A of the Rome Cemetery.

Private James L. Smith
29th Connecticut Volunteers
Age: 22
Height: 5'11"
Birthplace: Camden, New York
Occupation: Farmer

If James Smith had never enlisted we would never had any knowledge of this young man. Fortunately, the United States Military kept records.

Before his enlistment, Smith lived with his parents and siblings on a farm located in Camden. Three weeks before Christmas of 1863, he enrolled at Hartford, Connecticut, for three years in the 29th Connecticut Volunteers. At his enlistment on December 4, Smith was given the rank of fourth corporal. On April 30, 1864, he was reduced to the rank of private and never attained a higher status again.

From April until August of 1864, the 29th Connecticut was stationed at Beaufort, South Carolina. On August 8th, the unit moved to Virginia where it participated in the operations against Petersburg and Richmond. Private Smith was present during these movements, which included numerous battles. His regiment was the first infantry regiment to march into the fallen city of Richmond on April 3, 1865.

After the Virginia campaigns were over, the 29th went to Maryland to guard prisoners and then sailed to Texas for more garrison duty. On October 24, 1865, Smith mustered out of service in Brownsville, Texas, and was honorably discharged at New Haven, Connecticut, on November 25, 1865.

With Smith's discharge from the Army, he vanishes from the written pages of history. Undoubtedly, he returned to Camden and his family, but of this, we have no further documentation.

Private James A. Williams
29th Connecticut Volunteers
Age: 24
Height: 5'4 ½"
Birthplace: Madison, New York
Occupation: Boatman

James Williams embarked on his military career at Hartford on January 2, 1864, in Connecticut's first colored regiment. The unit was organized at Fair Haven from January to March 1864. In March of 1864, they left for Maryland, then were sent to South Carolina, and were finally sent to Virginia and participated in the siege of Petersburg and Richmond.

As part of the 29th, Williams took part in numerous major battles: Deep Bottom and Strawberry Plains, August 14-18; New Market Heights, Fort Harrison, September 28-29; Darbytown Road, October 12; Fair Oaks, October 27-28; and then before Richmond until its fall on April 3, 1865. Unfortunately, Williams was detached as a teamster and was unable to share the honor of being the first infantry regiment to march into Richmond. On July 3, 1865, Williams was discharged for disability.

Before the war, Williams worked on the Erie Canal. While loading a team of horses on the boat "*Clinton,*" the animals bolted into the water, and Williams went into the canal to drive them up the bank. While doing so, a horse lunged forward striking his leg. He was taken to Rochester where his broken limb was set. He was then sent to the Utica City Hospital for about 3 months. All of this, combined with his military activities, contributed to his physical handicap over the years.

Returning to Utica after the war, he worked at the A. E. Culver Store, Dickinson & Comstock store, and upon the canal docks. He lost the use of both his legs in 1893, thus becoming totally disabled. On December 13, 1903, he was dropped from the pension rolls because of his death. During his lifetime, Williams was married twice and lived at 14 Post Street. His first wife, Mary Conway, of Clinton, died July 13, 1890. He remarried Rorella Titus in June of 1891. Her death date is not known.

54TH MASSACHUSETTS VOLUNTEER INFANTRY

Private Cornelius Harding
54th Massachusetts Volunteers
Age: 41
Height: 5'4"
Birthplace: Hagerstown, Maryland
Occupation: Barber

Cornelius Harding enlisted in the 54th Massachusetts Volunteer Infantry the same day as C. W. Lloyd and Norman Knox. These three Uticans traveled and enrolled together. There is documentation that these men were close friends.

Training occurred at Readville, Massachusetts, before the journey south began. Harding fought through the battles of Fort Wagner on Morris Island, South Carolina, July 18, 1863; Olustee, Florida, February 20, 1864; Honey Hill, South Carolina, November 30, 1864; and numerous other skirmishes. After serving over two years, his regiment mustered out on August 20, 1865, at Charleston, South Carolina, where Harding opted to have $6.00 deducted from his pay to retain his rifle and equipment.

When Harding arrived home, his health had been ruined. Fellow veterans James Williams and C. W. Lloyd attested to this for the Bureau of Pensions on his behalf. Complaints of rheumatism, a bad heart, and swollen limbs plagued him until his death on February 23, 1893. His remains are in the New Forest Hill Cemetery in Utica.

Harding married twice. His first wife, Diane died (date unknown), leaving him to raise two sons and one daughter. The boys were: Henry, 12 years old; Edward, 6 years old; and daughter Emma, 9 years old. He remarried on December 11, 1891, to Mary Carter of Utica. When Widow Harding applied for her pension benefits, she had declared that her "worldly possessions amounted to not more than $20.00 in value and no ownership of realty."

Private Wilbur Jackson
54th Massachusetts Volunteers
Age: 16
Height: 5′9″
Birthplace: Fort Plain, New York
Occupation: Barber

Wilbur Jackson is an enigma in military history. The U. S. government said he did not serve in the military. Jackson and several friends stated that he *did* serve in the 54th Massachusetts Volunteer Infantry and the 26th United States Colored Troops during the Civil War.

Jackson reportedly first enlisted in the 54th Massachusetts, then transferred to the 26th United States Colored Troops on September 4, 1863, at Schenectady, New York. He was then sent to Hart's Island, and from there, proceeded to Virginia and later to South Carolina. While traveling by ship, he fell on an overcrowded deck and broke his arm. After being released from the hospital, Jackson went to duty at Beaufort, South Carolina, until his discharge on September 4, 1865.

In 1870, Jackson moved to Utica to become a valued resident. Jackson worked as a cigar maker until 1875, when he opened a saloon on Post Street where he lived. Also known as "Shad," Jackson's clambakes were reportedly superior to anyone else's in the state. His services were in great demand. The nickname came from a type of fish he served at his clambakes.

During the early 1880's Jackson applied for a government pension stemming from his injury aboard the troopship. This was promptly denied on August 5, 1892, there was no extant record of him serving in either regiment. About a year later, on June 25, 1893, he passed away suffering from typhoid pneumonia. His remains were returned to Fort Plain, New York, for burial on June 27, 1893.

Jackson was a respected colored citizen of Utica who was sorely missed. While alive, he was a member of the Reynolds Post, Grand Army of the Republic, the Knights of Pythias, and the Roscoe Conkling Lodge. Although denied his benefits because of the lack of military records, his being a member of a G. A. R. Post offers credence that he did in fact, serve his country.

The Late WILBUR JACKSON

Private Wilbur Jackson's portrait was taken from his obituary in the *Utica Saturday Globe*, Saturday, July 1, 1893. Jackson reportedly served in the 54th Massachusetts Volunteers and the 26th United States Colored Troops. The government had no record of his military service. Nicknamed "Shad" because of the fish he served at his superb clambakes. Jackson also was a member of the Reynolds Grand Army of the Republic Post.

Private Norman Knox
54th Massachusetts Volunteers
Age: 20
Height: 5'8"
Birthplace: Cooperstown, New York
Occupation: Boatman

Knox, of Utica, was a third bona fide member of the 54th Massachusetts Volunteer Infantry from Oneida County. As with his friends, Harding and Lloyd, he enlisted the same day and followed the same course as they did.

Two days before the assault of Fort Wagner in Charleston Harbor, South Carolina, on July 16, 1863, Knox participated nearby in the first skirmish of his regiment with Confederate forces on James Island. This fight was recreated in the movie "Glory." On February 20, 1864, Knox once again participated in the clash of arms at the Battle of Ocean Pond, also known as Olustee in northern Florida. Though a Union defeat, the 54th again proved its value as they held off the rebel forces during the Union retreat.

Knox later served detached duty as a teamster and was mustered out August 20, 1865. During his term of service, Knox was fined $21.25 for the careless loss of his Enfield musket and accoutrements. This was almost 2-months pay. Returning to Utica, Knox lived with his mother Ann for a time, and then disappeared from the area.

Private Charles W. Lloyd
54th Massachusetts Volunteers
Age: 20
Height: 5'3"
Birthplace: Whitestown, New York
Occupation: Laborer

On April 9, 1863, Charles Lloyd (also spelled as Loid) enlisted in Readville, Massachusetts, in what became the most famous of all the colored regiments during the Civil War—the 54th Massachusetts Volunteer Infantry. Lloyd performed duty as a drummer with the regimental musicians. He served in this capacity at the battles of Fort Wagner, South Carolina, and Olustee, Florida. When not using his drum in the engagement, he served as stretcher bearer. Both of the battles were Union defeats, but each showed the fighting character and the value of this Federal black unit. In both fights, Lloyd was under severe fire while performing his duty.

After mustering out in August of 1865 in Charleston, South Carolina, Musician Lloyd returned to Utica. When he returned to civilian life, he became a hostler and minister at the Hope Chapel Church. He filled this position until his death on July 21, 1919, at his 6 Dewey Avenue residence in New Harford. Lloyd was also employed as a notary public.

Lloyd married twice. His first wife, Julia Fox was Caucasian and died June 7, 1894, at Utica. His second wife was a colored woman, Maria Hollenbeck, who died July 13, 1936. A pension was allotted because of diseases contracted while Lloyd helped construct water batteries during the siege of Charleston.

The Reverend Musician Charles W. H. Lloyd now lies at rest with hundreds of comrades at Utica's Forest Hill Cemetery in the Veterans Memorial Section.

55TH MASSACHUSETTS VOLUNTEER INFANTRY

Private Henry Charles
55th Massachusetts Volunteers
Age: 18
Height: 5'7"
Birthplace: Peterboro, New York
Occupation: Farmer

Madison County native, Henry Charles, enlisted for military service on June 15, 1863, at Readville, Massachusetts. Charles joined the 55th Massachusetts Volunteers. This unit was formed from the overflow of their sister regiment from the Bay State, the 54th Massachusetts.

On July 21, 1863, the 55th left the state for the Carolinas. Upon reaching its destination, the 55th was placed on fatigue and active duty. The 55th took part in numerous actions which included Morris Island, August 9 – September 5, 1863; operations around Charleston and Fort Sumter, September 17 – October 25, 1863; campaigning in Florida, February – April 1864; Honey Hill, South Carolina, November 30, 1864; and numerous expeditions and skirmishes in South Carolina until the War's end. On August 29, 1865, the 55th was mustered out at Orangeburg, South Carolina. The regiment was officially discharged at Boston, Massachusetts, on September 23, 1865.

While serving with the 55th, Private Charles was detailed as a teamster in November of 1863 and as a mounted orderly in June of 1865.

Charles returned to Madison County after the war. On April 28, 1868, he married Sarah Davis. In 1889, the Charles family was living in Rome, New York. The exact dates of the Charles' residency in Rome are not known. In Rome, he worked as a laborer performing odd jobs. On May 27, 1922, Charles passed away, and he was interred on May 29, 1922, at Peterboro Cemetery.

A Grand Army of the Republic photograph exists which shows and substantiates Henry Charles as a G. A. R. member. The photo is undated, but appears to be around the turn of the century and was taken on the Peterboro village green.

Private Henry Charles
Co. F, 55th Massachusetts Volunteer Infantry

117TH NEW YORK VOLUNTEER INFANTRY

Officers' Servant Robert Wilson
117th New York Volunteers
Age: 28
Height: Unknown
Birthplace: Culpeper, Virginia
Occupation: Slave

Robert Wilson was perhaps the only unofficial soldier of color to serve both sides during the war. "Uncle Bob" was born a slave on August 1, 1833, at his master Albert Tutt's plantation in Virginia. In 1861, Wilson accompanied his master to the war as a wagon driver.

Wilson became free when Union forces occupied his master's farm. Traveling to Fort Baker, Washington, DC, he attached himself as a personal valet to Major Rufus Daggett of the 117th New York Volunteer Infantry and came to Utica with the major when the war concluded.

Known as "Bob" or "Uncle Bob Daggett," he worked on a farm for a while, then in a hardware store in Syracuse. Later in life, Wilson returned to Rome as a coachman for R. M. Brigham.

On August 1, 1869, he married Christiana Van Dusen from which two sons, Edward and Albert, and two daughters, Ida Mae and Georgiana, were born. Wilson later worked as a barber. He died in February of 1937.

Wilson was so popular with his adopted 117th New York Regiment that he was invited to all of the reunions. He attended the 50th anniversary at Camden and went to the Blue & Gray reunion in 1907 at Wilmington, North Carolina. Regimental Historian of the 117th, George B. Fairhead, stated: "Always best & proper in dress & manners. He could most accurately reproduce Col. Daggett's tone, voices and manner of giving command." He was extremely popular.

"Uncle Bob Wilson" was born a slave, and for a time, was a wagon driver in the Confederate army. Wilson later escaped the Union lines and was the personal servant for Major Daggett of the 117th New York Volunteer Infantry. When the 117th New York Volunteers returned home at the war's end, Wilson came with it and settled in Rome, New York. *(Courtesy of the Rome Historical Society)*

Colored Laundress Marie Hunter. Hunter served for the officers of the 2nd New York Heavy Artillery. Her photograph was found with some photographs of Captain Morven M. Jones, 2nd New York Heavy Artillery. *(Author's Collection)*

Sub-Cook Bedant L. Baird
16th New York Heavy Artillery
Age: 45
Height: 5'6"
Birthplace: Western, New York
Occupation: Farmer

Three days before Christmas of 1863, Bedant Baird enlisted in Co. K, 16th New York Heavy Artillery as an undercook of African descent. Baird retained his status for his entire enlistment and did not transfer to the United States Colored Troops, as did the Pell brothers *(see pages 42,58,104)*.

Baird served his regiment faithfully in his support capacity with the Army of the James. In nearly a year and a half of service, Baird saw action in Virginia during the Siege of Petersburg and Richmond, July 17, 1864 – January 3, 1865; Dutch Gap Canal, August 16; Strawberry Plains, August 14-18, Chaffin's Farm, September 28-30; Darbytown Road, October 13; the expedition and capture of Fort Fisher, North Carolina, January 4-15, 1865; the capture of Wilmington, North Carolina, and various duties around North Carolina.

With the cessation of hostilities, the 16th was ordered back to Washington, DC, in July 1865. On August 21, 1865, Baird was mustered out with his regiment. From Washington, Baird returned to his native town of Western. Once again reunited with his wife, Julia, and children, he resumed farming.

In the years following his return, the family moved to Whitestown. Baird died there on November 10, 1891, from the effects of exposure during the war, the cause of death being chronic rheumatism and heart infection. Julia Baird continued living in Whitestown drawing her Government pension until her death on October 9, 1903.

Sub-Cook Charles H. Peterson
16th New York Heavy Artillery
Age: 30
Height: 5'4"
Birthplace: Western, New York
Occupation: Farmer

Charles Peterson began his military life on December 28, 1863. His official mustering in took place in Utica on January 4, 1864. Peterson actually enlisted as a private, but never served in that capacity. For a year and a half, his rank was "Under Cook of African descent."

Sub-Cook Peterson served in the 16th New York Heavy Artillery faithfully during his regiment's services in the siege and battles outside of Petersburg and Richmond. He also took part in the campaigns in North Carolina in 1865. On August 21, 1865, Peterson mustered out with his regiment at Washington, DC.

Several years after his return to Rome, Peterson's first wife, Malvina Anderson, died in either 1869 or 1872. From this union, a daughter, Malvina, had been born. On February 7, 1874, Peterson remarried Mary Barberich. To this second marriage was born five more children: Charles, 1873; Edith, 1874; Hiram, 1876; Aggie, 1877; and John, 1892.

The family moved to Auburn, New York, around 1874 where they joined the Zion Colored Church. Pastor Thomas did not believe that they were legally married, so he performed another marriage ceremony before their admission to his church.

As with most Civil War veterans, Peterson applied for a government pension. War time diseases interfered with his livelihood as a laborer and the pension was finally granted.

On November 7, 1899, at the age of 57, Peterson died of fever and tuberculosis. His wife, Mary, after re-submission for benefits, continued to receive his benefits until her demise. The date of her death is unknown.

14TH RHODE ISLAND COLORED HEAVY ARTILLERY

Private Henry Howard
14th Rhode Island Colored Heavy Artillery
Age: 44
Height: 5'5"
Birthplace: Harford County, Maryland
Occupation: Laborer

Howard was one of the first recruits for the 14th Rhode Island. He signed up on October 15, 1863, for three years' service. Howard endured the drudgery of army life in Louisiana until October 2, 1865. On this date, he mustered out and returned to civilian life once again. the only thing notable among his military events was the losing of his governmental gear, which he contested. The exact year of Howard's arrival in Clinton is not known, but it was in the 1870's.

As with other surviving veterans of the 14th Rhode Island, he suffered from chronic diarrhea and rheumatism during his service years, which lasted the rest of his life.

Howard performed manual labor until so impaired by his infirmities, that he found it necessary to collect a government pension. He began collecting $8.00 a month, which was later increased to $12.00 a month.

Little much else is known of Howard's life except that his wife's name was Jane, and that they were preceded in death by a six-month-old son named George H.

Howard passed away on February 28, 1897, at the age of 80. The Howard family was laid to rest in the Old Burying Ground in Clinton in the right corner of the cemetery at the entrance.

Corporal William H. Labiel
14th Rhode Island Colored Heavy Artillery
Age: 20
Height: 5'8 ½"
Birthplace: Vernon, New York
Occupation:

During the first two years of the war, thousands of Oneida County sons left their homes to put down the rebellion. The county quickly sent off two regiments, the 14th & 26th New York Volunteer Infantry, to the front lines. Both of these units suffered severely during their term of service. Shortly afterward, the 97th, 117th and 146th New York Volunteer Infantry took the field to defend the nation. Oneida County also sent units of artillerymen, engineers and cavalrymen plus another 100 or more sailors to the conflict. All of these men had one common goal and all of them were Caucasian.

Upon the announcement of Lincoln's Emancipation Proclamation that took effect on January 1, 1863, the recruitment of soldiers of African descent began in earnest. Oneida County also answered this call. Colored volunteers first left the area in the spring of 1863 to enlist in some of the first black regiments raised in the northeast. About 50 colored men left for the war from the county. This was a rather large number for an upstate locale.

Cornelius Harding, Norman Knox, and Charles Lloyd left Utica, traveled to Readville, Massachusetts, and enlisted in the newly formed 54th Massachusetts Volunteer Infantry. Several other area colored men enlisted in the 29th Connecticut Volunteer Infantry while at least 8 more went to Providence, Rhode Island, where they mustered into the 14th Rhode Island Heavy Artillery. This unit was later federalized and became the 11th United States Heavy Artillery. The 11th served mainly in Louisiana doing garrison and patrol duty. Another small group joined the navy while the balance entered the Regular United States Colored Regiments.

William H. Labiel of Vernon was one of these early colored volunteers. At the age of 20, Labiel signed up in Syracuse and then traveled to Providence, Rhode Island, where he mustered in on

December 17, 1863, in the 14th Rhode Island Heavy Artillery. A short time later, William's younger brother, Lewis, age 18, enlisted in the 31st United States Colored Troops at Hart's Island, in New York Harbor. This regiment was the third unit that was organized in the state of New York.

Labiel was enlisted as a musician. He left behind his father Henry, age 52, and mother Harriet, age 51. The family also consisted of three brothers and one married sister, Mary Rogers, age 29. William's three brothers were: Lewis, age 18; Charles, age 7; and George, age 4. Labiel affectionately referred to his siblings as Loo, Charly and Georgy in his letters home.

Private William Labiel trained at Dutch Island, Rhode Island, then in February of 1864, he was promoted to the rank of corporal by order of Colonel Nelson Viall. On May 1, 1864, he was reduced to the rank of private for unspecified reasons.

On February 6, 1864, a silk standard was donated to Labiel's 3rd Battalion by the colored ladies of New York City. The flag had the arms of Rhode Island on one side and the coat of arms of the United States on the other. This battalion did not sail immediately for New Orleans because of an outbreak of smallpox. Finally on April 3, 1864, the detachment sailed on the ship *Daniel Webster* for New Orleans. It took ten days to reach the city, from which they were ordered to Camp Parapet as part of the defenses of the Crescent City.

Captain Henry Southwick (14th R. I. C. H. A.) stated: "the fort at Post Parapet was a massive work, and a line of heavy earthworks called the Parapet extended from this fort to the New Orleans and Jackson Railroad, that ran not far from the edge of the swamp. Along this railroad were small picket posts with a stronger detachment at the Pass. Beyond and east of the railroad were lighter earthworks, and a tall lookout tower constructed of timber, was situated near the Metaire Ridge Road, a back way, as it were, into the City of New Orleans from the North. Camp Parapet was on the comparatively open and dry territory south of the Parapet proper. Here were barracks of unpainted lumber."

Garrison duty occupied most of Labiel's time with few skirmishes and no battles with the Confederate forces. While stationed here, he trained at the cannons every fourth day for three hours. This was done until perfection was achieved. The signal to "man the guns" was three rapid taps on the bass drum, repeated with intervals of five seconds – three times.

During his stay in the deep South, he became severely ill with chronic diarrhea, which ultimately led to his demise. William suffered for weeks from this malady until the end. He died on August 4, 1864, at the Corps D'Afrique Hospital in New Orleans were he also was buried never to return to his beloved home in Vernon. Upon his death, Labiel's close friend, Sergeant William H. Johnson, notified his family of the sad occurrence. Johnson survived the war and mustered out with the unit on October 2, 1865.

The 14th Rhode Island finished its service in Louisiana and returned for a farewell parade in New York City, and then traveled to Providence where it was paraded once again and mustered out on October 21-23. While in the service of the United States, they lost three men killed and scores to disease. Several other Oneida County men died in this outfit from chronic diarrhea.

What makes William Labiel especially interesting is the fact that he and his family could write during these times. Almost all of the county's colored soldiers could not write or even sign their name. An "X" was their mark made for their signature. Labiel wrote home frequently and his family responded in like manner.

Many people know of the Civil War through the diaries, letters and books of the average white soldier. A colored man's thoughts on the war, national events, and everyday hopes are quite unique.

Several years after William's death, his father applied to the Commissioner of Pensions for a pension. Henry declared that both of his sons who were soldiers had supported him because he was an invalid. Their mother, Harriet, had passed away on November 20, 1872. A pension was granted to Labiel at a rate of $8.00 per month. In 1880, the father turned the letters over to his attorney, George C.

Carter of Utica, who in turn submitted them to the pension office for proof for an increased rate of $12.00 a month. Also included were two letters from William's Sergeant, informing of his death. These letters were kept by the pension office and are now held at the National Archives in Washington, DC.

Corporal Labiel offers a rare insight on the daily life of a local Oneida County colored solider in his letters. The spellings, the grammar and the lack of punctuation are normal for the common Civil War soldier when conveying his messages anywhere. Labiel shows emotions and his hopes for the future after military service. He recognizes the value of an education and emphatically reminds his mother to keep after brothers Georgy and Charley. As now, money is a major concern of his because of his future plans for a new house for his parents. This dream did happen, but the property was in care of his sister Mary. Unfortunately William would never see if his dreams came true.

The letters have been copied in the same form as they were originally written. Labiel always capitalized important words to him, especially the word write, which he spells "Rite." How many letters Labiel actually wrote and sent, we will never know. What ever happened to the photographs he had posed for is another mystery. From surviving accounts and records, a sketchy description of him can be drawn. He was 20 years old, 5'8 ½" tall, with black eyes, black hair and had an African complexion. He wore a blue uniform with red stripes on the pant legs and a kepi with crossed cannons and the Company letter K on it, and a cape. He was quite well attired for a young soldier who carried an imported .54 cal. Austrian musket, handled the cannon when needed, and the desire to uphold his regiment's mottos: "FREEDOM TO ALL, DEATH TO COPPERHEADS AND TRAITORS!"

His letters that survived are a vivid testimony to a young black soldier's life in the 19th century and help us appreciate the colored soldiers' contributions to a largely prejudiced area.

On the following pages are a few of Labiel's letters located in the National Archives, Washington, DC.

Duches Island R. I.
Dec 20th 1863

My Dear Mother
And Father

The opportuneity has at last came and I feel it my duty to Rite to my dear and effectionate parents, To them that has brot me up this period of time, and I never can pay you for what you have both done for me, but i feel indeted to you for wat you have done for me. I am well and hoping this letter may find you all well. I got a letter from Mary. It went to Syrucuse and friend of mine broat it to me.

Mother, have you got a check for 50 dollars that came in a letter from Rhode Island as i sent, and if you did not get it, Rite and let me know just as quick as you get this. I am inlisted in Rhode Island for 3 years, and got 50 dollars and sent a check. We are going to get 175 dollars, and if you get the first i sent, i will send you the rest of it in a short time. And to my dear little Charley and Georgy, Kiss 100 times for me and do not let him for get me. Tell Bailey that i am well and Mrs. Bailey my love and all my friends.

Mother, do not for get and Rite as soon as you get this and let me know about that check, and do not for get it, and if you have not got it, i will get another one, and you can get money out of any Bank you want to. It is dinner time and i must stop. I will rite moore about our funn in my next letter. My love to all~~

Direct your Letter
Wm H. Labiel Providence
Rhode Island
14th Reg Hevy Artillery
Co. K in care of
Captain Barney

From your Sun
William H. Labiel
Providence R. I.
14 Reg Hevy Artillery
Co. K   Rite Soon~~

Duches Island
Dec 30 1863

Dear Sister

The opportuneity is at hand, and I feel it my duty to Rite to you. I am well and hope this letter may find you well Sister Mary. I am in the Army. I left Syracuse a month ago and inlisted. I got 75 dollars bounty and sent fifty dollars to ma, and we are to have 175 when we leave Rhode Island. I received your kind letter on the 20th and was glad to hear from you for i have not see you for 2 years that i know of. You would not know me. I will send my picture, but the cloak I cannot send, but i would willingly send it if i could, but as it is now, I can not. Adam, your Cosin is here and John Lewis from Schoharie is here, and we have lots of funn. Father and mother do not know where i am. I shall rite home to day.

Mary Please Rite Soon

Direct William H. Labiel
Providence Rhode Island
14 Regiment Hevy Artillery
Co. K

To Mrs. Mary J. Rogers
From William K Labiel
Providence R. I.

Duches Island
Feb 13 1864

Dear Mother, Father
Your letter of last month I received, wich contained 2 postage stamps, I was glad to here from you all. Ma, we shall soon be in New Orleans or Texas. I do not know wich, but we shall leave here soon, and my Bounty i shall have sent home. You will get it in the corse of 2 monts or sooner, and you must rite and let me know wether you get it or not. We shall not get it until we leave here, and i shall Rite to you agane before long, and you must Rite and let me

know all about the Bounty, if you get it or not, and all of the news. There will be $2.00 and i want to here from you and let me know if you have got it or not. I am well. I Weight 156 pounds. I will send you my likeness as soon as i can get where it can be taken. Kiss Charley for me, and Georgy. Ma you must keep my money for me, and when i get home, we will bild a new house. I will send my money just as soon as i get it. I shall be worth 500 dollars when i get home. You must not think i will not come, for i will be home in a short time. 3 years will soon pass away. You must not get discouraged. Keep up good spirit. Make Charley go to school every day, so when I come home, i can see how much he has learned. You wanted to know if Loo could come down here to in list. Do not let him cause the Regiment is full, and if he coms, he will be transfurd in some other Rigement, and then you can not hear from him. Let him stay to home.

My love to all and Mary

Rite as soon as you get this.

> Direct Corprel
> W. H. Labiel
> 14 Regt. R. I. Hevy Artilry
> Company K
> Duches Island
> > Providence R. I.

Ma, i am Corp. in Co. K, and ware stripes on my legs. I order all of the boys.

~~~~~~

<div align="right">
Duches Island
March 10th Inst
</div>

Dear Mother,

I now ocupie this opportunity in Riteing to my dear Mother and Father and [am] happy to inform you both that i am well and enjoying good helth and hope you are the same. I rote to you that i wer goin to leave here, but there is so much sickness here now, that we could not leve. The transport has been here and gone back to New York. 'The Colonl thinks this Batalion will go by the way of land, and if we do, i shall come home before we go to New Orleans. All of the offersers *[officers]* of this Batalion says it is the best drill companys they ever saw.

There is 8 cases of the Small Pox on this Island, but all have been vaxenated and Warlked Balley and me. Onley one case died with it, and that one died this morning of March 10th. Other wise we are all well. Ma, you must keep Charley in school and have him learn all he can and if Loo has not inlested, you keep him at home, and if he has inlisted, he is not in this regt. They have taken him in the Masschusett Regt. or the Connecticut Regt., and he can not get his Bounty unless they have a mine *[mind]* to give it to him. My Bounty will be home; if not at home now, you need not be the least bit worred about it. You will get it and maby not until we get to our place of Destination. It will come and it is bound to come. Give my regards to all and to Olever Cassett and all of the boys. Kiss Georgy and Charley. My Regards to Bailey and family. Tell them i am well and received his and Charley letter.

> My address is
> Corpril W. H. Labiel
> 14 Regt. R I Hevy Artellery
> The Noble, Company K
> Duches Island
> Providence RI

Rite Soon
From Corp. W. H. Labiel
    your Son

~~~~~~

> La.
> New Orleans
> Camp Paripet
> June 6 1864

Dear Mother

Will you Rite to me? I am at present and doing well. My love to all. No Battles yet. I have been very sick. You would not know me if you see me. My hand is not right for a pen yet. I do not do any duty. I have not much to say this time. Rite soon. Kiss Charley for me. Keep him in school. Let me know where Loo is.

From W. H. L.
My address
Corp. W. H. Labiel
14 Regt. R. I. H. A. Co. K
Camp Paripet
New Orleans La.

If i get an answer from this i have a check to send to the amount of 75 dollars

Rite Soon   Send me some postage stamps

~~~~~~

Camp Paripet
New Orleans

Dear Mother and Father

And againe I Rite to you to let you know i am well and alive. Hope this letter may find you all the same. It is some time since you hurd from me, but it is very busey times here now, and we do not get time to Rite much. I am happy to Rite to you that i never was better in helth in my life. The wether is very warm here, but it just suits me. Dear Mother, it is now the time when i can feel the love of you that has broat me up to the presant time. I know you and Pa are geting old and had aut *[ought]* to have the attension of those you have broat up, and for me, i shall do all i can to keep you comforible all tho i am mehny miles from you, but do not think, but that i shall come home agane. We are in good conditions, have lots of funn and all we want to eat and drink, and that all I could get if i was at home. There is oney 30 monts yet to serve. It will soon pass away. Ma, when you Rite, let me know if you have received $150 of my bounty and let me know in the next letter; and if you get, put it in the Bank of Vernon. And if you want to use the $50 dollars, you use it, and if you dont want it, why you leve in the bank. Be shure and keep Charley in school and let him get a good edduction *[education]*, and when he gets to be as old as i am, it will be a use to him. Kiss him for me. My regards to Mrs. Brown. Rite some news—let me know every thing that is goin on. My love to Mary.

> My Address
> Corp. W. H. Labiel
> 14th Regt. R. I. H. Artillery
> Company K 3rd Battillion
> New Orleans   La.
> Camp Paripet

~~~~~~

> Camp Paripet
> Near New Orleans La.
> August the 11th 64

Parents of
    William H. Labiel

Sorry am i to sit down to inform you of the death of your son Wm., who departed this life August the 4th at the General Hospital in New Orleans & I have just received information of his death.

We miss him very much, and he was esteemed and respected by all who knew him and was a faithful soldier to his duties as a soldier.

He was sick for about 3 weeks before he was sent to the Genl. Hospital and was getting better & looks the same, but as we was ordered to move, the sick had to be sent to the Hospital untill health would permit them to be sent on to the battallion.

We as brother Comrads of Company K do all feel the effect of the loss of our comrad & share a portion of your grief.

This is from a friend of W. H. Labiel,

> Sergeant Wm. H. Johnson
> Company K, 11th U. S. H. Artillery

Camp Parapet New Orleans LA.

Please answer soon & let me know wheather you rec. this.
Direct to me as above.

~~~~~~

<div align="right">

Camp Paripet
Near New Orleans, La.
Nov. the 5 1864
</div>

O. Carpenter Esq.
   Dear Sir

   Yours having just come to hand, and in which I gladly
hasten to answer as reguards [to] the effects of my deceased friend,
Wm Labiel.

   The Bank that was to be paid to him by the state of R. I. was
$250, two hundred and fifty dollars of which he received the full amt.

   Before he went to the Genl. Hospital, I think that he sent his
check home to his folks as it would do him no good here, for I
believe that he had his checks made out in the name of his parents at
Vernon, and the check was to be cashed [by] them. So he could not
have had any money on his penson at the time of his death other than
the check.

   There was some three months pay due him from the
Government besides some back pay.

   This is all. This will be sent on to his parents next pay day.
We have not been paid yet in six months.

  This from a friend
  Sergt. Wm. H. Johnson
  Co. K. 11th U. S. H. Arty
  Camp Parapet
  New Orleans   LA.

11TH UNITED STATES COLORED HEAVY ARTILLERY

Corporal Amos G. Freeman
11th United States Colored Heavy Artillery
Age: 23
Height: 5'7 ½"
Birthplace: Utica, New York
Occupation: Laborer

Freeman began his military service at Providence, Rhode Island, on November 21, 1863, in the 14th Rhode Island Heavy Artillery—Colored. Leaving behind a wife and two children, he trained at Dutch Island, Rhode Island, until April when his battalion sailed for New Orleans.

While in training on February 17, 1864, Freeman was promoted to corporal. Freeman was present with his regiment until July, 1864, when he came down with typhoid fever. On August 4, 1864, after several weeks of suffering with the fever, Freeman expired at the regimental hospital at Camp Parapet, Louisiana. Another Oneida County soldier, Corporal William Labiel of Company K of the same unit, also died on that day.

At the time of his demise, Freeman's only personal affects where his clothes and one blanket. Nothing further is known of his family after his death.

Private George Hall
11th United States Colored Heavy Artillery
Age: 18
Height: 5'4"
Birthplace: Washington, DC
Occupation: Farmer

George Hall was another citizen of Oneida County to enlist in the 14th Rhode Island Colored Heavy Artillery. Hall mustered in on November 23, 1863, at Providence, Rhode Island. After several months of duty in Rhode Island, the regiment was sent to New Orleans for garrison duty.

No battles occurred around the Crescent City for the 14th to take active part in during their stay. On October 2, 1865, Hall was mustered out of service and was officially discharged at Providence. Hall retained his musket and accoutrements, being charged $6.00.

Before the war, Hall was a resident of the town of Westernville. Upon his discharge, he returned to Oneida County. On December 17, 1874, he married Susan A. Frank in Rome. The ceremony was performed by the Reverend W. F. Heurenway. The family resided here for the rest of their lives with Hall being wracked by diseases related to his military service. Rheumatism, diarrhea, fevers and general debility plagued him. Following the paths of other ex-soldiers, Hall applied for a government pension in the early 1890s.

During this era, Hall worked sporadically as a coachman until his death on November 17, 1902. At this time, the family was living at 610 Mercer Street.

Susan Hall was dropped from the pension rolls upon her death on October 8, 1913. One child, Jessie H. Hall, is known to have survived the couple.

Private Andrew Jackson
11th United States Colored Heavy Artillery
Age: 24
Height: 5'4"
Birthplace: Unknown
Occupation: Laborer

Jackson enrolled on October 22, 1863, at Providence, Rhode Island, in the 14th Rhode Island Colored Heavy Artillery. After leaving the state, Jackson performed the dull life of garrison duty in New Orleans. He was the only man in the 11th United States Colored Heavy Artillery from Oneida County that we know of, that had a harrowing counter with Confederate forces.

Captain Addeman described the sad incident:

"in the midst of these rumors of attacks, in the early morning of August 6th, we were visited by a body of mounted men. They dashed upon our pickets who made a bold stand for a short time, and then scattered for shelter. The rebels had caught sight of the Lt. Aldrich who was in command and while a part of them made diligent search for him, the remainder dashed into the town, and breaking up into parties, raided through the various streets, firing somewhat indiscriminately, but more particularly at what contrabands they saw. The companies gathered in their respective bastions in the fort and was expecting a lively brush. As the rebels did not appear to be coming to us, a strong detachment under command of Adj. Barney, was sent out to exchange compliments with them. They gave us no opportunity for this, but soon retired, taking with them three of our pickets and one cavalry vidette, whom they had captured. We understand, the next day, that our men were shot in cold blood. Lt. Aldrich, and the men with him, escaped through the friendly protection of an orange Osage grove. Others swam the bayou, and thus escaped certain death or being captured. I think our casualties were, besides those taken prisoners, on e man killed and four wounded. Several of the rebels were said to be killed or wounded."

The rest of Jackson's enlistment was uneventful. He mustered out with his regiment on October 2, 1865. From Rhode Island, he returned to Oneida County.

Jackson resumed working as a laborer in various locations of Westernville, Utica, and Rome. On August 18, 1876, Jackson married Mary J. Frank of Westernville. The Reverend Wilson B. Parmlee of the Presbyterian Church of Westernville performed the ceremony. This was Jackson's third marriage. His previous spouses were both deceased.

When Jackson first applied for a pension, he was 63 years old. From his #14 Burnet Street address in Utica, he claimed total disability. A gunshot wound to his right leg, rheumatism, partial deafness, and rupture all took a toll on the aged veteran.

No proof of the gunshot wound could be found in the military service records. As far as it is known he was never granted a pension. On September 9, 1897, Jackson passed away.

Some time in the 1890's, the family moved to Rome, New York, where Jackson's widow continued her pursuance for a pension. The date of her death is not known. No children were born of this marriage.

Private Levi Palmer
11ᵗʰ United States Heavy Colored Heavy Artillery
Age: 20
Height: 5′7″
Birth: Whitestown, New York
Occupation: Laborer

Palmer started his lengthy military career on October 22, 1863, at Providence, Rhode Island. From here, Palmer and his regiment traveled by ship to New Orleans where, for almost two years, he did garrison and picket duty. A few skirmishes relieved the boredom of this station until his muster out on October 2, 1865.

Returning home, Palmer worked as a laborer until the formation of two new colored cavalry regiments that were being raised for service on the western plains. Upon learning of these new regiments, Palmer traveled to Carlisle Barracks, Pennsylvania, where he enlisted in the 10ᵗʰ United States Cavalry on August 1, 1867.

Palmer was sent to Fort Leavenworth, Kansas, where he became Oneida County's first "Buffalo Soldier." The name was given to these men of color by the Great Plains Indian tribes. For the next five years, he traversed the Plains which were the most violent and unstable area of the United States. The 10ᵗʰ Cavalry saw active service fighting Indians, lawless banditti, guarding railroads, as well as general military duties. Trooper Palmer mustered out on August 1, 1872, at Fort Sill in Indian Territory (present day Oklahoma) with the endorsement of his Colonel as a man of good character.

For three years, he remained a civilian. On March 26, 1875, Palmer again enlisted, this time in the 25ᵗʰ United States Infantry, which, like the 10ᵗʰ Cavalry, was all black except for the officers. Back to Texas went foot soldier Palmer to resume escort and guard duty with occasional Indian fights. When his five-year enlistment expired, he was a physical wreck. The rough life of soldiering had taken its toll. An aged Palmer entered the Soldiers & Sailors home in Quincy, Illinois, where he spent the remainder of his life. During his stay, he was plagued by a bad heart, rheumatism, syphilis, piles and general fatigue. Palmer died on May 21, 1918, and was buried at the home's cemetery. He never married.

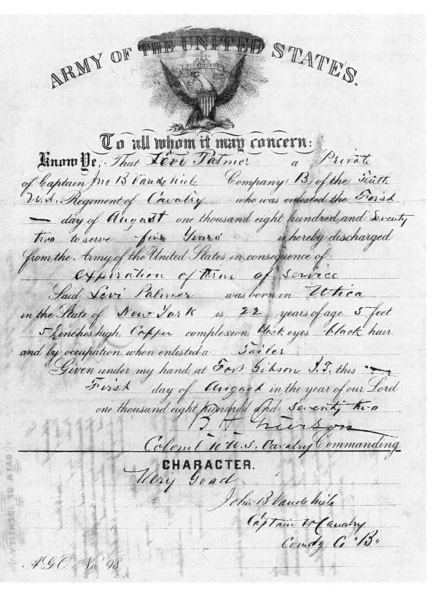

Discharge Paper of Private Levi Palmer, Company B, 10th United States Cavalry. Palmer served in the 11th United States Colored Heavy Artillery during the Civil War. *(Author's Collection)*

Sergeant John Pell
11ᵗʰ United States Colored Heavy Artillery
Age: 26
Height: 5'10"
Birth: Whitestown, New York
Occupation: Waiter

John Pell was born in 1837 and was the son of Joseph and Margaret Pell. Susan Murphy of Schoharie became his wife on December 21, 1859. Pell had two other brothers in the service, James and Prince Albert, who served with Co. D of the 10ᵗʰ United States Colored Troops. This was the only colored family of Oneida County to have three brothers serve.

Pell worked as a laborer and waiter at the City Hotel and the Dudley House. In 1860 and 1862, two daughters, Martha and Grace, were born. At the time, the family resided at 15 Charlotte Street. The Pells were quite a large family in the City of Utica for that period. On November 14, 1863, Pell traveled to Providence, Rhode Island, and enlisted in the colored 14ᵗʰ Rhode Island Heavy Artillery. This unit served in Louisiana doing garrison duty. Pell was promoted a corporal in the Color Guard on December 31, 1863, and promoted a Sergeant July 6, 1864. Both promotions were ordered by the colonel of the regiment.

The 14ᵗʰ suffered only a few casualties from the Confederate forces during their tenure in the South. Disease was the primary enemy, and this caused the death of Sergeant Pell on November 1, 1864. His remains were buried at Camp Parapet, Louisiana. After his death, his wife Susan received a government pension with $2.00 a month added for each of their two daughters. This extra allowance expired upon each daughter's sixteenth birthday.

On February 11, 1872, Mrs. Pell died and was buried in Utica's Potters Field. The orphaned children were then under the guardianship of various people until reaching the age of 16. One of the guardians was Supreme Court Justice William J. Bacon whose only son, William Bacon, Jr., with the 26ᵗʰ New York, who had been killed in the war at the Battle of Second Bull Run, in August, 1862. The children finally went to live with their grandmother, Martha Jackson.

Private William W. Smith
11th United States Colored Heavy Artillery
Age: 45
Height: Unknown
Birth: Annsville, New York
Occupation: Farmer

Smith was one of the older colored men to serve the Union cause from Oneida County. Born on May 19, 1818, he was 45, not 23, as he claimed at the time of his mustering in at Providence, Rhode Island.

Smith joined the all colored 14th Rhode Island Heavy Artillery on November 18, 1863. Traveling with the 14th, Smith spent most of his military tour in Louisiana. During his enlistment, he reportedly broke his leg servicing an artillery piece. He finished his time with the regiment and mustered out on October 2, 1865, in Rhode Island.

When he got back to Camden, Williams returned the life of a farmer. His first wife was Mary Benton of Florence. Her date of death is not known. Smith then remarried on July 4, 1891, to Roselle Leonard. He had no children by his first marriage, but fathered one son and three daughters by the second.

In May, 1928, Smith lost his home to a fire. With the help of friends, he was able to rebuild a new home and resume his life.

On October 2, 1931, after a short illness, death claimed Smith, affectionately known as "Uncle Bill Smith," at the old age of 113. As with many veterans in his area, Smith had joined the Grand Army of the Republic. He was a member of Skillen Post 47, Rome, New York. Post records for October 3, 1931, show the following entry concerning his death: "Death of Comrade William Smith reported and it was decided to attend the funeral and perform the usual service. Motion made and carried that the Commander hire a Taxi to attend funeral of Comrade Smith."

Private John D. Thomas
11th United States Colored Heavy Artillery
Age: 27
Height: Unknown
Birthplace: Lewis County, New York
Occupation: Unknown

Thomas enlisted in the 14th Rhode Island Heavy Artillery in November of 1863. Beyond this 1865 New York State Census fact, his life is a mystery.

There were two John Thomas' in the 14th. The first enlisted in October of 1863. He was 21, born in Delaware County, Maryland, was single and was a member of Company E. He died in the battalion hospital of dysentery on September 6, 1865, at Donaldsonville, Louisiana.

The second Thomas was 19 years old and born in Salem, New Jersey. He was a member of Company H and was promoted to the rank of corporal in August, 1865. Thomas mustered out on October 2, 1865, at New Orleans.

No pension file exists for either of these men. Only one military file exists at the National Archives. Yet, Rhode Island state records hold only one file, which is a different man from the federal records.

The New York State Census of 1865 states these facts on Thomas. They are as follows: "Camden – 2nd District – Mulatto – age 22 – born Oneida County – servant – husband – Private – 14th Rhode Island November 28, 1863. This information is on page 15 line 38 and 39."

Sergeant James M. Wells
11th United States Colored Heavy Artillery
Age: 25
Height: 5'4"
Birthplace: Frankfort, New York
Occupation: Laborer

Wells was the eldest of two brothers who entered military service during the Civil War. The older Wells chose the army while the other brother joined the navy. On October 30, 1863, he signed up in Providence, Rhode Island, but was not mustered in until January 25, 1864.

Within a week of joining the regiment, he was promoted from private to sergeant. Wells retained his stripes until his muster out. Besides his promotion, he was also assigned to the Color Guard of his regiment. His new position was one of great honor and danger as the Color Bearers were often the first casualties in battle.

On March 21, 1865, he received a pass to visit the nearby city of New Orleans for the day. Wells did not return until the morning of the 23rd and was promptly arrested for being absent without leave. Wells was brought up on the charge on April 19 and found guilty. He was fined $10.00 of one month's pay. This was extremely lenient, as in most cases, he would have lost his rank.

Upon his mustering out in October 1865, Wells exercised his option to retain his weapons for a price from the government. He undoubtedly proudly returned home in his uniform carrying his Austrian musket and non-commissioned officer's sword. No further information is known about Wells.

Private Frank Wilson
11ᵗʰ United States Colored Heavy Artillery
Age: 28
Height: 5'7 ½"
Birthplace: St. Louis, Missouri
Occupation: Laborer

Wilson was a resident of Jordan, New York, when he enlisted in the 14ᵗʰ Rhode Island Colored Heavy Artillery. He enrolled on December 7, 1863, and was mustered in on December 31, 1863.

After completion of its organization and training, the 14ᵗʰ was sent to the New Orleans area. Here it did garrison duty around the environs of the city with a very monotonous existence. The 14ᵗʰ lost its state identity and became known as the 11ᵗʰ United States Colored Heavy Artillery. Wilson was assigned daily duty in his Company "L" as company cook. Company records show him present until the expiration of his term of enlistment. The regiment was mustered out on October 2, 1865, at New Orleans. Wilson opted to buy his musket and equipment for $6.00 at this time.

Some time after the war, the Wilson family moved to Rome, New York, to live. Wilson performed manual labor which was interrupted by sickness contracted during the late war. As with many ex-soldiers of this era, Wilson filed for a pension. On February 15, 1884, he passed away with his interment two days later in the Rome Cemetery. Several years after his death, a clouded chapter was opened during pension claims.

During January, 1886, Elizabeth Wilson of Rome, New York, applied for a widow's benefits of her late husband. She stated that she had married him on November 13, 1879, in Rome by the Reverend B. Wingate. Her maiden name was Elizabeth Thomas. In June of 1890, a second wife, Sarah, entered the pension picture. She claimed that she had married Wilson on January 15, 1858, in Elbridge, New York, by Justice of the Peace Bullock. Her maiden name was Sarah Jane Van Schaick. Sarah won out in the bid of a pension. On June 20, 1923, she died in Jordan, New York, and was officially dropped from the pension rolls on July 4, 1923.

1ST & 40TH UNITED STATES COLORED TROOPS

Private John Green
1st & 40th United States Colored Troops
Age: 20
Height: 5'7 ½"
Birthplace: Hanover Court House, Virginia
Occupation: Farmer

John Green enlisted as a private in the 1st United States Colored Troops on February 14, 1863, at Mason's Island *(now Teddy Roosevelt Island)*, Washington, DC. From Virginia, the 1st United States Colored Troops traveled to the Carolinas and participated in an expedition from Norfolk, Virginia, to Camden Mills, North Carolina. The regiment then returned to Virginia and participated in assaults and the Siege on Petersburg. In the latter part of 1864, the 1st was sent back to North Carolina. On January 15, 1865, the Union forces, with the help of the Colored Troops, successfully captured Fort Fisher at the mouth of the Cape Fear River. They then took part in the capture of Wilmington, Goldsboro, and the surrender of Joseph Johnston's Army at the Bennett Place near Durham.

On February 12, 1865, Green was discharged at Folly Island, South Carolina, because of two gunshot wounds to his left leg—one between the knee and the hip, and the other in his left foot which he had sustained at Folly Island on July 25, 1863. In November of 1866, Green re-enlisted in the 40th United States Colored Troops, which was stationed in North Carolina until his discharge February 20, 1869. He was discharged upon the recommendation of his company commander as being "utterly worthless as a soldier and a confirmed malingerer." Upon his release of military duties, he came to Utica and boarded on 67 Water Street and later on Genesee Street.

It is not known if Green was married. In 1897, Green applied for a government pension because of total disability from his wounds. He was almost prosecuted for fraud when another John Green (alias Henry Jones), who served in the same outfit, tried to apply for the pension. Green's attorney (Rouse Maxfield of Utica) abandoned the petition for pension late in 1897, probably because of Green's death, although his passing away was not confirmed.

1ST UNITED STATES COLORED TROOPS

Sergeant Robert Jackson
1st United States Colored Troops
Age: 20
Height: 5'7"
Birthplace: Troy, New York
Occupation: Barber

In May of 1863, the United States Army began recruiting the 1st United States Colored Troops. This was one of the first official Colored Federal Infantry regiments not organized from a state unit.

May 19th was the first day of enlistment for the regiment. On this day, Robert Jackson of Utica enlisted at Washington, DC, one of the first recruits for this newly created outfit.

Almost immediately, Jackson was sent on detached service to Portsmouth, Virginia. At this time, he held the rank of sergeant. While on duty, Jackson went absent without leave for a time and was placed under arrest. On June 26, 1863, he was reduced in rank to private and had to forfeit $5.00 of his pay, as well as pull ten days of hard labor living on bread and water.

Jackson served with the 1st at the following battles and skirmishes: Camden Court House, North Carolina, December 5-24, 1863; Butler's operations south of the James against Petersburg and Richmond, Virginia, May 4 – June 15, 1864; Wilson's Wharf, May 24, 1864; the Siege of Richmond and Petersburg, June 16 – December 7, 1864; the Mine Explosion at Petersburg, July 30, 1864; Chaffin's Farm, September 27-30, 1864; Fort Harrison, September 29, 1864; Fair Oaks, October 27-28, 1864; various expeditions and the final assault and capture of Fort Fisher, North Carolina, January 7-15, 1865; Sugar Loaf Hill, January 19, 1865; Capture of Wilmington, February 22, 1865; and the Campaigns in the Carolinas.

On March 21, 1865, Private Jackson deserted near Faisons, North Carolina, where his regiment was on active campaigning.

Jackson returned to his unit around May 26, 1865. No court-martial proceedings were found for his flagrant conduct. Regimental returns for June 26, 1865, show that Jackson was discharged while the regiment was in North Carolina. He mustered out on September 29, 1865.

Little is known of Jackson except that his mother, Ann, was married to Joseph Gordon, age 37. Jackson was from his mother's first marriage. A sister, Ida Gordon, age 12, lived in Utica with the family. Besides this scant information, most of Jackson's life remains a mystery.

1st United States Colored Troops, in which Sergeant Robert Jackson and Private John Green served. Circa November 1864. (Courtesy of the Library of the William G. Hamilton Archives, University of Massachusetts.)

Magnified views of previous photo of the 1st United States Colored Troops, circa November 1864. *(Courtesy of the Leonard A. Walle Collection at the United States Military History Institute)*

3RD UNITED STATES COLORED CAVALRY

Private Eli Baylis
3rd United Sates Colored Cavalry
Age: 28
Height: 5′5 ½″
Birthplace: Richmond, Virginia
Occupation: Slave and Field Hand

Of all the Oneida County Colored Veterans, Eli Baylis had the most interesting and exciting military career that was as dangerous as any of his white comrades.

Baylis was born around 1835 on the Baylis Family Plantation near Culpeper Court House, Virginia. His early years were spent working in the Baylis cotton fields, and the fields of his next owner named Jenkins. Jenkins was a cruel master which caused Baylis to run away. After being chased by dogs and recaptured, he was branded with a hot iron on the thigh.

With the outbreak of the war, Baylis made good his escape and finally reached the sanctuary of Union territory. Once here, he supposedly enlisted in a heavy artillery regiment, but no proof could be found to support this. On October 18, 1863, Baylis did enlist in the 1st Regiment Mississippi Cavalry which became the 3rd United States Colored Cavalry.

The newly formed 3rd patrolled the military districts of Mississippi and parts of Tennessee. This unit participated in numerous major campaigns in that area such as: Roach's Plantation, Haines Bluff, Yazoo City and vicinity (4 times), Utica, Mississippi; Goodrich Landing, Fort Adams, Gaines Landing, Arkansas; Big Black River Bridge, Egypt Station, and Franklin, Tennessee; as well as operations to capture Jefferson Davis near Irwinville, Georgia

Baylis served as a private his entire enlistment, acting as a blacksmith, artificer (a skilled craftsman who could repair regimental equipment), and saddler. While in service, he broke the little finger of his left hand and suffered from the various maladies typical of the era. On January 26, 1866, he was honorably mustered out at Memphis, Tennessee.

In 1867, he moved to Albany, New York, and then to Rensselaer County. While living there, he married Sarah Lavender who bore him two daughters. Baylis worked for 20 years at the coalyard of Ham & Cook and then moved to Utica in 1906. The Baylis resided on both Elizabeth and Catherine Street while in the city. The veteran died of "old age" on September 11, 1911. He was 75 years old. Baylis left behind his wife Sarah and two daughters, Mrs. Hattie Williams of Hamilton, New York, and Mrs. Sarah Blair of Utica, New York.

Baylis was laid to rest with his fellow veterans at the Soldiers & Sailors Memorial section the in Forest Hill Cemetery in Utica, New York.

4TH UNITED STATES COLORED TROOPS

Private George Thompson
4th United States Colored Troops
Age: 15
Height: 5′8 ¼″
Birthplace: Oneida County, New York
Occupation: Farmer

Private Thompson is one of the County's mystery colored soldiers. According to the Census of 1865, George lived in the 2nd Ward with his 49-year-old father, Isaac. Thompson served with the 4th United States Colored Troops for four months from May of 1863 until August when he was discharged because of his age. He had claimed he was 19, when in reality he was only 15. Being very tall, he lied about his age and was believed.

No federal, state or pension records could be found on this aspiring young soldier. This leaves us with a soldier of military service who was one of several other county Blacks who remains virtually unknown because of poorly kept records on all levels. The only mention of a George Thompson that could be found was in the *Utica Daily Observer*, February 1, 1864, and this was in relation to several robberies that occurred in the Rome area. Though, because of the time span and dates, it is believed that this is not the same youth.

8TH UNITED STATES COLORED TROOPS

Private Milton Frank
8th United States Colored Troops
Age: 21
Height: 5'7"
Birthplace: Oneida County, New York
Occupation: Farmer

Frank enrolled in Utica on August 26, 1863, in the United States Colored service. Frank was one of several colored citizens from Oneida County to be drafted. In Philadelphia, Pennsylvania, Frank was assigned to Company G, 8th United States Colored Infantry.

As a member of the 8th United States Colored Troops, Frank fought at the Battle of Olustee, Florida, on February 20, 1864, and was wounded. He was sent to Beaufort, South Carolina, to recuperate. He rejoined his regiment in May of 1864. Frank participated in more active service. On September 29, 1864, he was once again wounded, this time at the Battle of Chaffin's Farm, Virginia.

Frank ended up at Lowell General Hospital, Portsmouth Grove, Rhode Island, where he died in January of 1865. Two dates, January 20th and 30th, were given for his death. Government records stated his death was caused by heart disease. New York State Census records of 1865 list his death was caused by wounds.

The final resting place of Frank is not exactly known, but he most likely was interred on the grounds of the Lowell General Hospital where he passed away.

Private Garrett S. Russell
8th United States Colored Troops
Age: 21
Height: 5'9"
Birthplace: Peterboro, New York
Occupation: Laborer

Garrett Smith Russell, who was named after famous abolitionist Gerrit Smith, enlisted in the United States service on August 31, 1863 at Oswego. After being sent to Elmira, Russell was assigned to a detachment of recruits for the 8th United States Colored Troops. This outfit was being organized at Camp William Penn in Philadelphia.

The 8th United States Colored Troops left Philadelphia on January 16, 1864, for Hilton Head, South Carolina. After a two-week stay, the regiment was transferred to Florida. There, the 8th United States Colored Troops saw its first battle, The Battle of Olustee, which was a Union defeat. The 8th suffered 310 casualties, including the commanding officer, but acquitted itself honorably.

From Florida, the unit was sent to Virginia where it fought at Bermuda Hundred, Chaffin's Farm, Darbytown Road, and the Siege of Petersburg. The regiment also was present at the fall of Petersburg and the pursuit of Lee's army to Appomattox. On May 24, 1865, the 8th sailed for duty to Texas. Here they were stationed at Ringgold Barracks and along the Rio Grande. In November of 1865, the regiment returned to Philadelphia where it was mustered out of service.

Russell was present during all of his regiment's tour of duty. On May 1, 1865, he was appointed Principal Musician. A month later, he was court-martialed for an unknown infraction and was fined $5.00. On June 29, 1865, Russell was promoted to the rank of sergeant. He held this position until his mustering out on November 10, 1865. At this time Russell elected to purchase his sword and accouterments as souvenirs.

With the war's end, Russell returned to the Madison and Oneida County area. On April 17, 1869, he was married to Kitty Martin in Waterville. The marriage was performed by Reverend E. Davis of the Congregational Church.

The Russels moved to Clinton about 1871. Here, Russell worked for Dr. Gartner of Hamilton College and Dr. Oren Root. Root's son, Elihu, was Secretary of State at this time. The couple owned a small house on the banks of the Oriskany Creek.

In the late 1880's, the veteran's war years took their toll. Incapacitated by diarrhea, rheumatism and a bad heart, Russell was granted a Federal Pension. On June 1, 1891, he was able to collect $6.00 a month, which he did until his death, and thereafter, his wife.

Russell died of stomach cancer November 24, 1906, at the age of 64. He was buried at his birth place in Peterboro, New York. His wife, Kittie, lived in their home until her death in 1912. His daughter, Jessie, born November 5, 1886, survived the couple.

10TH UNITED STATES COLORED TROOPS

Private James Pell   **Sergeant Prince Albert Pell**
10th United States Colored Troops & 16th NY Heavy Artillery
Age: 24   **Age: 21**
Height: 5'8 ½"   **Height: 5'6 ½"**
Birthplace: Whitestown, New York
Occupation: Common Laborer   **Occupation: Farmer**

In Utica, during the time of the Civil War, resided three brothers who enlisted in the Union army. These three soldiers were James, Prince Albert, and John Pell. Sergeant John Pell served with the 11th United States Colored Heavy Artillery. *(Read about the third Pell brother on page 42.)* The brothers were born in Whitestown. Their parents Joseph and Margaret Pell moved to Utica in 1855 and resided on Post Street. Various members of the Pell family lived on this street for 50 years. *(See photo on page 106.)*

Both James and Prince Albert enlisted in Company I of the 16th New York Heavy Artillery in Utica, New York—Prince on January 2, 1864, and James on January 4, 1864. The Pells enlisted in a white regiment as cooks and servants. They carried water, cooking and performed other camp duties. After almost two years of service with the 16th, James and Prince Albert transferred on April 28, 1865 to the 10th United States Colored Infantry, which was a black unit with white officers.

Life was better for the Pells in the new outfit. While stationed in Corpus Christi, Texas, James was detached for duty with the Quartermasters Department, and later as an orderly in the Inspector Generals Office. James remained a Private until his discharge May 17, 1866.

Prince Albert fared better. In August, 1865, he was promoted to corporal, then sergeant in March, 1866. He mustered out the same day as his brother.

Both men did see a small amount of action during the Siege of Petersburg with the 16th. The Pell brothers did their Patriotic duty, and received $302 bounty for enlisting. The Pells returned to their families in Utica shortly after the war. James and Prince Albert were both married in 1859 though they continued to live with their parents.

Prince Albert resumed working in the city as a Coachman for John S. Peckman—a job he did for 11 years. His first wife died in 1871. Prince Albert remarried in 1873 to Catherine Page. He filed and received a government pension because of fever, ague, and piles contracted while in the service. Prince Albert died on September 23, 1894, while he was visiting in Richfield Springs, New York. His body was returned to the city and buried September 26, 1894 at New Forest Cemetery. His wife, Catherine, died August 6, 1902.

James Pell returned home and worked as a gardener and any other odd and end jobs he could find. Sickness from Civil War service continued to affect Pell. In 1880, James applied for a pension. Malarial poisoning, fever and rheumatism plagued the veteran. The worst affliction he had at this time was mental illness. He succeeded in receiving his pension, but was dropped from the rolls in 1882. In 1884, James was confined in the Utica jail. While in jail, James said he saw angels and the apostles and that he spoke with these spirits. Judge Sutton of Oneida County declared him to be a chronic case of "religious insanity."

James' wife, Nancy, applied again for a pension but was denied, the medical examiner stating his mental condition was not service related. James remained an inmate of the State Lunatic Asylum in Utica until 1886. He then was transferred to the Insane Department of the Alms-House in Rome, New York. While here, he was kept hand-cuffed, as he was "inclined toward violence and very boisterous in prayer." In 1909, at age 69, James Pell died from a cerebral hemorrhage, and is buried in Lot 12 of the New Forest Cemetery.

It is truly a sad ending for two of Utica's first colored soldiers—one from physical and the other from mental disorders.

Captain Oliver W. Sturdevant
10th United States Colored Troops

A native of Verona, New York, Sturdevant originally was a member of the 44th New York Volunteer Infantry and fought at the battles of Antietam, Fredericksburg, Chancellorsville and Gettysburg. Passing General Silas Casey's examining board of officers of colored regiments, Sturdevant was appointed captain in the 10th United States Colored Troops. The Pell brothers, Prince Albert and James, were members of this unit. Sturdevant resigned from the army on April 1866 at Galveston, Texas. (From *A History of the 44th Regiment, New York Volunteer Infantry* by Captain E. A. Nash)

16TH UNITED STATES COLORED TROOPS

Private Foster Johnson
16th United States Colored Troops
Age: 18
Height: 5′4″
Birthplace: Miami County, Ohio
Occupation: Farmer

Foster Johnson enlisted in the 16th United States Colored Troops on September 12, 1864, at Dayton, Ohio. From Dayton, Johnson was forwarded to join his regiment at Chattanooga, Tennessee. The 16th participated in the Battle of Nashville on December 15-16, 1864; Overton Hill, December 16th; and the pursuit of General Hood's Army to the Tennessee River, December 17-28, 1864. Then the regiment was posted at Chattanooga once again, and later, in various areas of the state.

On September 14, 1865, Johnson was honorably discharged at Chattanooga. When he left the service, he opted to retain his Enfield Rifle and accoutrements for the price of $6.00. Johnson, assumedly, returned to Ohio where he married Rachael Kimball. She died June 16, 1892, at Xenia *(pronounced Zena)*, Ohio.

Some time in the mid-1890's Johnson came to Rome, New York, where he met and married Ida May Wilson on July 12, 1895. From this marriage, two sons were born—William on January 16, 1897, and Robert on October 24, 1899.

As with many veterans, Johnson applied for and received a pension for rheumatism and swelling of the right leg incurred during his military service. Johnson died in Rome, New York, on September 3, 1903. His remains were laid to rest at the Rome Cemetery. The death date of Mrs. Johnson is not known.

20TH UNITED STATES COLORED TROOPS

Private Abraham Schuyler
20th United States Colored Troops
Age: 19
Height: 5'6"
Birthplace: Utica, New York
Occupation: Laborer & Barber

Few facts are known about Abraham Schuyler except for his short military career. Schuyler enlisted on August 31, 1864, in Utica with a group of volunteers for the Colored Regiments. When he arrived at Riker's Island in New York Harbor, he was assigned to the 20th United States Colored Troops along with several other colored recruits from Oneida County.

Private Schuyler traveled with his unit through its garrison duty in Louisiana and Florida until his expiration of service on August 30, 1865.

After his military obligations were over, Schuyler drops from public notice. The last thing found mentioning him, is a pension deposition by Oneis Van Dusen—a United States Colored Troops veteran. Van Dusen stated that he had served with Schuyler in the same company of the 20th United States Colored Troops, but that this man was now dead. The deposition was given in 1892.

Private Henry Simmons
20th United States Colored Troops
Age: 35
Height: 5'6"
Birthplace: Canaan, New York
Occupation: Farmer

Henry Simmons of Florence left his wife, Mary, and their three children on September 5, 1864, to serve his country. Upon his arrival in Utica he enlisted in a "detachment of U. S. Volunteers to be forwarded for U. S. C. T. and Riker's Island, N. Y. H." Once he arrived there, he became a member of the 20th United States Colored Troops.

Simmons was forwarded to Camp Parapet, Louisiana, and then to Florida. During this journey, he broke his right foot and was hospitalized from January to June of 1865. Approximately half of his enlistment was spent in the hospital. Returning to the 20th United States Colored Troops in July of 1865, Simmons performed garrison duty until his mustering out with the regiment on October 7, 1865, at New Orleans.

After his discharge, Simmons did not return to Oneida County, but instead moved to New York City. From there, he moved to Albany and went back and forth until he settled in Schaghticoke, Rensselaer County. Still not content in one place Simmons moved to Springfield, Massachusetts.

Simmons had two more children later in life, both girls. In 1887, his wife Mary whom he married in 1852, passed away.

How Simmons made a living after the war is unclear. His broken leg and foot bothered him as did kidney disease and heart problems. He did collect a pension from the late 1880's until his death. The old veteran died April 11, 1919. His remains were brought back to Schaghticoke for interment. Upon his death, Simmons left no estate, only unpaid bills to the amount of $594.00. Interestingly, the two daughters, Cordeillia and Isadora, submitted a nursing care bill of $400.00 for their services in their father's final weeks of life.

Private Bradford Tompkins
20th United States Colored Troops
Age: 18
Height: 5'6 ½"
Birthplace: New York, New York
Occupation: Laborer

On August 28, 1864, at age 18, Bradford Tompkins enlisted at Norwich, New York, as a recruit for the United States Colored Regiments. On October 26, 1864, Tompkins was officially placed on the muster rolls of the 20th United States Colored Troop at Hart's Island, New York Harbor.

Two months after his initial enlistment, young Tompkins was promoted on Christmas Day to the rank of Corporal. In March of 1865, while stationed at New Orleans, he was again promoted to first sergeant, but by a special order on November 22, he was reduced to the rank of private on May 8, 1865.

During his enlistment, Tompkins served in Florida, Louisiana, and Texas. His time was mostly spent on garrison and patrol duty. On August 28, 1865, he mustered out at Milliken's Bend, Louisiana. Tompkins returned North after his discharge and lived in Jamestown, New York. On December 24, 1874, Tompkins married Josephine Storm of Busti, New York. Four children were born from this marriage. They were Grace, Florence, Mildred, and William.

Around 1874-75, the Tompkins moved to Rome, New York. During the next fifty years, Tompkins utilized his skill as a barber and common laborer to support his family. The family lived on West Dominick Street. As he entered his golden years, he became unfit to work and was able to collect a government pension. Rheumatism, heart problems, hemorrhoids and vertigo all took their toll on the aged veteran. In 1924, the Tompkins moved to Roxbury, Massachusetts, and resided with their daughter Gertrude Houston. Tompkins died at his daughter's home on January 23, 1929. His remains were sent back for burial to Rome where the Skillen Grand Army of the Public Post No. 47 conducted services. Tompkins had been a member of this post. On December 8, 1933, Mrs. Tompkins passed away, also at her daughter's home.

Private Onius Van Dusen
20th United States Colored Troops
Age: 18
Height: 5'9"
Birthplace: Montgomery County, New York
Occupation: Drover

Onius Van Dusen enlisted on September 18, 1864, in Utica for the term of one year. His friend Abraham Schuyler of Rome enlisted with him at the same time. From Utica, Van Dusen was sent to Riker's Island and Hart's Island for training. His southward journey continued to Florida and New Orleans, Louisiana.

In January of 1865, Van Dusen was placed under arrest. General Order No. 8 Headquarters Southern Division, Louisiana, in February read: "Charge 1 'Assault,' Charge 2 'Robbery.' Finding Guilty. Sentence – To be confined at hard labor at such place as the comdg. Gen'l may designate for six months, with loss of all pay which may become due him for said period. Approved. Ft. Pickens, Florida designated as the place of confinement. By Command of Brig. Gen. Sherman."

The sentence commenced February 18, 1865, ending with Van Dusen returning to his regiment to finish his enlistment. During his imprisonment, he missed the military actions of his outfit and was mustered out on September 7, 1865. Despite his confinement, Van Dusen was honorably discharged to resume a peaceful life.

Immediately after the war, he returned to Rome. He moved to Syracuse and worked at the store of Ford & Butler for 12 years. While living there, he married Agnes Williams on May 29, 1873. Some time in 1885, Van Dusen went insane and was committed to the state asylum at Utica, and later at Binghamton. While confined at the Binghamton State Hospital, Van Dusen died of apoplexy and general paresis, at 10 p.m., June 28, 1887. His wife, Agnes, received her pension beginning in November 1890. By the time of her death in the 1930's, she was receiving $40 a month.

21ST UNITED STATES COLORED TROOPS

Two officers from Oneida County are listed on the 21st United States Colored Troops Memorial *(below)*. Lieutenant Colonel Augustus Bennett received the surrender of the city of Charleston, South Carolina, from its Mayor. The other Oneida County officer was Chaplain Erasmus W. Jones. Jones was a well known abolitionist, tailor, singer and songwriter. *(Courtesy of the Oneida County Historical Society.)*

Chaplain Erasmus W. Jones
21st United States Colored Troops
Utica Saturday Globe, January 16, 1909

Jones was a noted abolitionist before the war and hailed from Remsen, New York. During his lifetime, he was noted singer, abolitionist, lecturer, writer, preacher, temperance advocate, poet, and army chaplain during the Civil War. At age 91, Jones passed away on January 9, 1909, at his home in Utica, New York. He was interned at the New Forest Hill Cemetery in Utica, New York.

Private William Anderson
26ᵗʰ United States Colored Troops
Age: 37
Height: 5'7 ¾"
Birthplace: Oneida County, New York
Occupation: Farmer

William Anderson enlisted as a Private for three years in the United States Colored Troops on December 25, 1863, in Utica. From Utica, Anderson went with other area enlistees to New York Harbor for training. Here he was assigned with several other Oneida County men to Company F of the 26ᵗʰ United States Colored Troops. This company was commanded by Captain George England. England was also a Utican.

In April 1864, the 26ᵗʰ United States Colored Troops was ordered to South Carolina for active duty. Anderson was present for the expeditions to James & John's Islands July 2-10, action against Battery Pringle July 4-9, Burdens Causeway July 9, the Battle of Honey Hill on November 30, and several smaller actions in the month of December. After the completion of the 1864 Campaigns, the 26ᵗʰ was returned to Beaufort, South Carolina. Here from January to August of 1865, they performed garrison duty. On August 28, 1865, Anderson mustered out with his regiment at Hilton Head, South Carolina. He then returned to Utica.

Anderson resumed work as a farmer and common laborer. As he approached the golden years, his daily work schedule was often interrupted by rheumatism and chronic diarrhea. During the post war years, Anderson and his family settled in several areas of the state. They resided in Westernville, then Utica. From Utica they moved to Sterlingville and finally Felts Mills.

As with many veterans of this era, Anderson filed for and received a government pension. To help substantiate his claim he remarried his wife. She was the former Elizabeth Starnum who he had married before the war. The original date and proof of marriage was lost in both paper and forgotten in memory. Reverend Brown of Utica remarried the couple on November 29, 1884, in the city.

One son, Charles R., was born around 1860. The exact date is unknown. Elizabeth Anderson died February 10, 1902. Her maiden name was also given as Sharp. Anderson was dropped from the pension rolls on February 8, 1914, by reason of death. His burial took place in Sterlingville on February 10, 1914.

Private William H. Arch
26th United States Colored Troops
Age: 19
Height: 5'11 ½"
Birthplace: Long Island, New York
Occupation: Laborer

William Arch enlisted on December 28, 1863, in Utica as a member of a detachment of U. S. Colored Volunteers who were bound for Riker's Island in New York Harbor. Arch stated that he resided in the Fourth Ward of the City of Utica.

Originally, Arch was assigned to the 20th United States Colored Troops, but was sent to the 26th United States Colored Troops. On February 27, 1864, he was officially mustered into service at Riker's Island. In April 1864, the 26th was ordered to South Carolina.

The 26th spent its entire tour of duty in South Carolina. Here the Regiment took part in actions at James and John's Islands, Honey Hill, Devaux's Neck, Tillifinny Station and several other expeditions and skirmishes. Arch was present with his unit the entire time.

The 26th was mustered out on August 28, 1865, at Hilton Head, South Carolina. Arch decided to purchase his musket and equipment from the government and then returned home.

Arch moved to Chicago, Illinois, some time after the war. In Chicago, he was employed as a teamster until an old injury sustained in the military disabled him. Shortly before the war ended, Arch had been kicked in the left leg by an Army mule. This injury eventually led to him drawing a government pension for disability.

In 1885, Arch married Mary A. Donnelly of Chicago at that place. No children were born of this marriage. On November 30, 1901, Arch died of paralysis. It is not know when his wife died.

Private William J. Brown
26th United States Colored Troops
Age: 43
Height: 5'10"
Birthplace: Philadelphia, Pennsylvania
Occupation: Laborer

Little is known as to where William J. Brown lived at the outbreak of the Civil War. Military records show that he enlisted in the Town of Greenfield, Saratoga County, in February of 1865. The New York State Census of 1865 lists Brown as a resident of the Town of Florence, Oneida County. A possible reason for his enlistment in Saratoga County may have been the enticement of a $600 bounty.

Brown enlisted on March 11, 1865. He was sent to Hart's Island, New York Harbor, and then in June to Beaufort, South Carolina. Joining late in the war, Brown saw only garrison duty and was mustered out on August 28, 1865, at Hilton Head with his regiment.

After the War, Brown returned to Oneida County where he settled in Camden. There he worked as a common laborer until attacks of malarial fever and affliction of both eyes affected his work. His Regimental Surgeon had treated him for five weeks in July and August of 1865 for these medical problems.

Brown applied for a pension in 1885 after he went blind in his left eye. Limited vision and malarial attacks forced him to reside at the Soldiers and Sailors Home in Bath, New York.

A Watertown attorney by the name of Francis Fitch stated that his client, Brown, had died at the age of 76 in the Soldiers Home. No one wished to pursue his pension claim as the claimant left no widow or children. Brown's death had occurred in late 1886 and burial was presumably on the Home's grounds. Census records of 1865 state that Brown had been married twice.

Corporal Robert Glasby
26th United States Colored Troops
Age: 18
Height: 5'6"
Birthplace: Dutchess County, New York
Occupation: Laborer

Glasby (also borne as Glasbie) entered the United States service as corporal on January 6, 1864, in New York City. Being mustered in on February 27, 1864, at Riker's Island. Glasby was appointed corporal in Company F on the same day. On April 4, 1864, he was reduced to private, and the following October, he was restored to the rank of corporal. Glasby remained a corporal for the balance of his enlistment.

In April of 1864, the 26th arrived to Beaufort, South Carolina, for active campaigning. Their encounters with the enemy occurred in several skirmishes July 5 and 7, 1864, on John's Island, South Carolina. Later in the year, the unit was involved in more fighting at Honey Hill, South Carolina on November 30, 1864, and three additional engagements in December of 1864. The remainder of the regiment's service was peaceful duty at Beaufort, South Carolina, until mustering out.

Upon resumption of civilian life, Glasby married Sarah Grames on November 18, 1866, in Poughkeepsie, New York. Traveling around the state for work, he abandoned his wife and married Mary Van Alstyne on November 14, 1882, in New York City. A son, Robert Eugene, was born on October 7, 1886, in Utica, of this second union. Glasby worked as a janitor in Utica for several years until moving to Syracuse where he died December 2, 1896, and this is when the troubles began for his wives.

Both women filed for pension benefits. Neither knew about the other. After a thorough investigation, Sarah was pronounced the legal wife and Mary was a victim of Glasby's duplicity. Mary worked as a cook and lived in Utica on Elizabeth Street. A pension was collected by Sarah in Poughkeepsie until her death on March 7, 1924.

Private Henry Morrison
26th United States Colored Troops
Age: 35
Height: 5'9 ¼"
Birthplace: New Hartford, New York
Occupation: Laborer

Henry Morrison was born in 1828 and was a native of New Hartford where he enrolled. Morrison enlisted on December 28, 1863, for three years and trained at Riker's Island, New York. The regiment went to South Carolina were he fought in the battles of John's Island on July 7, 1864, and Gregory's Farm December 5 and 9, 1864.

Surviving these battles plus numerous skirmishes, Morrison mustered out on August 28, 1865, at Hilton Head, South Carolina, and returned to civilian life. Little else is known of him after that time.

Private Thomas Parker
26th United States Colored Troops
Age: 25
Height: 6'
Birthplace: Utica, New York
Occupation: Boatman

Native Utican Thomas Parker enlisted on January 4, 1864, as a member of the Colored Recruiting Detachment for the 26th United States Colored Troops. From Utica, Parker was sent to Riker's Island for training and then to South Carolina.

While in route to South Carolina, Parker deserted on April 8, 1864, at Annapolis, Maryland. According to the regimental records, Parker was "apprehended and arrested in Baltimore, Maryland, April 15, 1864. Rejoined the company for duty at Beaufort, South Carolina October 29, 1864. Took knapsack, canteen, and full set of equipment. There was $30 paid for his arrest and deducted from his pay."

Parker returned in time for the Battle of Honey Hill, South Carolina, on November 30, 1864. He then participated in actions at Devaux's Neck, December 6, Tilliffinny Station, December 9, and Mackay's Point, December 22, 1864. The Regiment then returned to Beaufort until its muster out on August 28, 1865, at Hilton Head, South Carolina.

Little else is known of Parker. From Census records of 1865, the schedule shows that he had a family. His wife, Olive, was 25 and his daughter, Ella, was eight years of age. No dates of death could be found for the veteran.

Private John Prime
26th United States Colored Troops
Age: 17
Height: Unknown
Birthplace: Oneida County, New York
Occupation: Farmer

John Prime is another colored soldier with a virtually untraceable background. Census records show this youth as a member of the 26th United States Colored Troops. No state or federal records verify this. Prime was born in Oneida County and lived in Utica with his father, William, and stepmother, Abigail. As with other mystery soldiers of the County, he most assuredly served but was given the wrong regiment of service when taken down by the enumerator of the district.

Private William J. Smith
26th United States Colored Troops
Age: 18
Height: 5'5"
Birthplace: Utica, New York
Occupation: Laborer

William Smith became a member of Co. F, 26th United States Colored Troops on Christmas Day of 1863 in Utica. He served under Captain George England, who was also a Utican. England was his company commander for the duration of Smith's enlistment.

Smith was sent to Riker's Island, New York Harbor, and then proceeded to the environs of Beaufort, South Carolina. Smith was reported sick from August of 1864 through April 30, 1865, at Hilton Head, South Carolina. Smith then returned to Oneida County after his mustering out.

Smith resumed doing manual labor to support himself. In 1879, the veteran applied for an invalid's pension through his attorney, George C. Carter, of Utica. Attorney Carter stated "on or about the 15th day of August 1864, he received and contracted inflammation of the brain which has caused the total loss of sight in his right eye and the partial loss of sight of his left eye, and that he so received and contracted said disease of the brain while he was with his command."

On December 18, 1895, Smith married Jennie Adsit at Rochester. She died at their home on July 9, 1903, of chronic hepatitis. Jennie was buried at New Forest Hill Cemetery, Utica. Smith married again on April 10, 1906.

His second wife was Isadore Willace of Utica. The ceremony took place at his home at 71 Water Street by the veteran soldier/ minister, Reverend Charles Lloyd. Isadore passed away on July 21, 1911, of cerebral hemorrhaging. No children were born from either marriage.

After the turn of the century, the semi-blind veteran did receive a full pension for the rest of his life. Death came to Smith on April 2, 1918. He was then laid to rest in Forest Hill Cemetery, Utica.

Private John H. Steenburg
26th United States Colored Troops
Age: 28
Height: 5'4"
Birthplace: Oneida County, New York
Occupation: Laborer

Not much is known of John Steenburg except for his military record. On Christmas Day, 1863, Steenburg enlisted in Albany in the United States Colored Troops. He was mustered in to service officially on February 27, 1864, at Riker's Island, New York Harbor.

Upon assuming active duty, Steenburg was assigned as a nurse in the Regimental Hospital. Steenburg held this position for most of his enlistment. Therefore he missed most of the units' active campaigning in South Carolina.

Private Steenburg was mustered out August 28, 1865, at Hilton Head, South Carolina with the regiment. Nothing else is known of his later life.

Private Peter Williams
26th United States Colored Troops
Age: 33
Height: 5'6 ½"
Birthplace: Auburn, New York
Occupation: Laborer

Williams was not a native of the Oneida County area before or during the war. His military services began on Christmas Day 1863 at Auburn, New York. After mustering in on January 4, 1864, Williams was sent with other colored recruits to Riker's Island, New York. Once there, he was assigned to Co. E., 26th United States Colored Troops.

In April of 1864, Williams' regiment embarked for Beaufort, South Carolina. During the fighting at John's Island July 2nd through the 10th, Williams was struck in the eye by a piece of exploding percussion cap off his musket. After being treated by the regimental surgeon, he was returned to his outfit. This eye plagued him the rest of his life. Private Williams was present during all of his units' battles until being mustered out on August 28, 1865, at Hilton Head, South Carolina.

Upon returning to Auburn, he married Caroline Adams on November 6, 1866. The Williams moved about looking for work and lived in Auburn, Elmira and Utica. Doing manual labor as a farmer and whitewasher, the family arrived in Utica in the late 1870's. The family resided at 17 Post Street until early 1885 when he died on March 22. "Neglect of health" was listed as the cause of death for this 56-year-old veteran. Mrs. Williams then returned to Auburn. In August of 1885, she had contacted her attorneys of Hoffman & Cook to proceed with processing her pension benefits. The widow Williams collected her pension of $8.00 a month until her death on September 18, 1901, at her Auburn residence.

Her husband Peter's remains lay in an obscure plot with a government headstone in the Forest Hill Cemetery, Utica.

Corporal Samuel B. Williams
26th United States Colored Troops
Age: 32
Height: 5'7 ½"
Birthplace: Oneida County, New York
Occupation: Boatman

Samuel B. Williams of Utica enlisted on December 8, 1863, in Utica. On the descriptive and muster roll of the United States Volunteers of Color for the 26th Regiment notes his actual first day of service was on December 18, 1863.

From Utica, Williams was sent to Riker's Island, New York Harbor for training. Within three months, he was promoted to the rank of Corporal. He maintained this rank until his muster out.

During this term of service, Williams participated in all of his Regiment's moves. The 26th was stationed in South Carolina where it took part in action at James & John's Islands, Honey Hill and numerous other skirmishes. On August 15, 1864, Williams was investigated for being absent from his Company. The charge proved unfounded. Corporal Williams served his enlistment out dutifully and was mustered out on August 28, 1865. This took place at Hilton Head, South Carolina.

Williams returned to Utica. He went to work for the firm of Hayes and Martin Grist Mill where he served as an engineer. The mill demanded hard work in which Williams was, at times, not capable of performing. He had contracted asthma in the Carolinas from exposure and thus earned a meager living.

In the late 1870's and early 1880's he applied for a government pension. At least four other colored veterans gave depositions for his case, but Williams was never granted a pension. On March 11, 1893, Williams passed away at age 63. During his lifetime, Williams was a member of the Utica Cemetery Association and appears never to have married. Because of his affiliation with the Cemetery Association, Williams was allowed to be buried with his white comrades in arms at the Soldiers and Sailors Plot in Forest Hill Cemetery. He lies in the front row.

31ST UNITED STATES COLORED TROOPS

Private George Carpenter
31st United States Colored Troops
Age: 37
Height: Unknown
Birthplace: Lysander, New York
Occupation: Laborer and Farmer

George Carpenter of Whitestown enrolled in Utica on August 4, 1864, to become a member of the United States Colored Troops. The middle aged farmer mustered into a detachment of United States Volunteers for Colored Troops on August 17, 1864, and was sent to Elmira. From there he was forwarded to Hart's Island, New York Harbor. On Hart's Island he was assigned to the 31st United States Colored Troops.

The 31st was already in the field on active campaign when Carpenter arrived. He participated in the 1864 battles of Fort Sedgwick on September 28, Hatcher's Run on October 27-28 near Petersburg, Virginia. In the spring of 1865, his regiment campaigned from the fall of Petersburg on April 2, to the surrender of Lee's army at Appomattox Court House on April 9, and then served in Texas until November of 1865. At Brownsville, Texas, Carpenter mustered out on November 7, 1865, and returned home.

Some time after the war, Carpenter and his wife, Wellthy, moved to Illinois. During the late 1880's, Carpenter applied for and eventually received a government pension. Although his military records show him present at all times, he claimed that he had been injured. He suffered from a rupture on the right side along with acute rheumatism. He was able to prove that he had been injured in the war and collected on the pension after several years. The injuries he sustained occurred in June of 1865 at New Orleans.

Carpenter died in Morris, Illinois, around 1897. His wife applied for a continuation of his benefits which she received until her death in March of 1909. The family was survived by at least one son, George Jr.

Private Daniel Dygert
31st United States Colored Troops
Age: 19
Height: 5'9 ½"
Birthplace: St. Johnsville, New York
Occupation: Laborer

Daniel Dygert enlisted in Utica on January 4, 1864, as a colored recruit for the United States service. Dygert, with a detachment of other colored men, was sent to Hart's Island, in New York Harbor, and assigned to the 31st United States Colored Troops.

In August of 1864, Dygert was sent to Virginia to participate in siege operations against Richmond and Petersburg. Dygert (or often misspelled as Daggett on army records) took part in the engagements of Weldon Railroad, Fort Sedgwick, Hatcher's Run, Bermuda Hundred, the fall of Petersburg, the pursuit of Lee's Army, and the surrender at Appomattox Court House, then finally, duty along the Rio Grande in Texas.

On February 1, 1865, Dygert was promoted to corporal, but in August, he was reduced back to private. Dygert mustered out on November 7, 1865, at Brownsville, Texas, and from there on, his life is a mystery.

According to the 1865 New York State Census, Dygert lived in the Fourth Ward in Utica. He had a 26-year-old sister, Joanna, and a nephew, Eli, age 6. In the Utica City Directory of 1864-65, a Mrs. Mary E. Dygert resided at 49 Charlotte Street. Possibly, she was Dygert's mother, and this might have been his residence also. Beyond this point, Dygert disappears from local records.

Private Robert Frank
31st United States Colored Troops
Age: 52
Height: 5'6 ½"
Birthplace: Amsterdam, New York
Occupation: Farmer

Frank had the shortest military career of any Oneida County colored soldier. He enlisted in Utica on January 4, 1864, from the town of Lee. Frank was forwarded to Riker's Island, New York for training, and before even being assigned to any of the regiment's companies, he met with an untimely death. While on guard duty on the night of March 16, 1864, he slipped off a wharf and fell into the East River. Before help could arrive, Frank drowned and his body was never recovered.

Mrs. Delano Frank moved to Rome, New York, where she collected her widow's pension of $8.00 per month, plus $2.00 per child of which she claimed five. A sixth child was too old to be claimed, being over 18 years old. The claimant died in December of 1876.

Sergeant Frances Henry
31st United States Colored Troops
Age: 23
Height: 5'8 ½"
Birthplace: Utica, New York
Occupation: Boatman

Henry enlisted on January 2, 1864, in Utica with a detachment of colored recruits to be sent to Riker's Island, New York. There, Henry was assigned to Company A, 31st United States Colored Troops, and was then sent to Hart's Island.

In April, the 31st transferred to the Army of the Potomac to guard supply trains during The Wilderness Campaign. From June of 1864 through April of 1865, the regiment took part in the Siege of

Petersburg. Henry was present during this period and was promoted to corporal on December 11, 1864, and made sergeant on September 8, 1865. In November, 1865, the regiment was in Brownsville, TX, where Henry mustered out on the 7th.

Census records from this period give Henry's age as 32. The fact that his wife, Louise was 35; and his son Daniel, 13; daughters Amelia, 16 and Ann, 12; support his age as 32, and not 23 as shown on his enlistment papers. Henry returned to Utica after the war.

During the Siege of Petersburg, Henry injured his ankle dodging a Rebel cannonball and later suffered from diseases contracted in Texas. Henry's friend, Alexander Jackson, described him: "he came home from the war in the fall of 1865. He was yellow looking, had trouble with his throat and cough on his lungs. He was all broken down." Working when possible, Henry suffered dearly until he could not work any more.

Sometime in the 1870's his first wife died, and Henry remarried Cora Boyd of Buffalo on March 18, 1890. The new Mrs. Henry was also previously married. Her first husband was an inmate at Auburn Prison where he was sent for second degree murder. The second wife left Henry in 1891. Although separated, Cora never applied for a divorce, but did apply for half of his pension.

Henry resided at 99 Liberty Street until his health forced him into the Soldiers & Sailors home in Bath, New York. in 1914. Meanwhile, his wife resided on Seneca Street in Utica. Both lived in Buffalo for several years in the late 1880's. On January 30, 1917, Henry died at the Veterans' Home in Bath. Henry is reportedly buried on the home's grounds.

Private Lewis Labiel
31st United States Colored Troops
Age: 18
Height: 5'4"
Birthplace: Vernon, New York
Occupation: Waiter

The military life of Lewis Labiel is rather confusing, as it involves four different Colored Regiments. On February 6, 1864, the eighteen-year-old Labiel enlisted in Vernon. His father gave the lad consent to sign up in January of 1864. At first, Labiel was to join the 14th Rhode Island Colored Heavy Artillery.

The recruitment papers were then changed to admit Labiel into the 26th United States Colored Troops. Upon arrival at Riker's Island, New York Harbor, he was assigned to the 31st United States Colored Troops.

Labiel served only about six months before being discharged for medical reasons. Prior to his enlistment, he suffered from epilepsy. The trials of military life increased the frequency of his attacks. At first, they struck about once a week, but they soon became almost a daily occurrence.

August proved to be a horrendous month for the Labiel family. By August 17, 1864, Labiel was discharged because of his pre-war disease. This was about two weeks after his older brother William's death in the 14th Rhode Island Artillery.

Labiel returned home for a short time. In February of 1865, he traveled to Norwich, New York, and enrolled in government service once more. From this time on, nothing more is known of Labiel as a soldier.

In June of 1869, Labiel died and was interred in the Vernon Cemetery on Cooper Street. Oddly enough, his headstone bears the legend of being a member of the 38th United States Colored Troops. Existing government records do not substantiate this.

Corp. James H. Sutphen
31st U. S. Colored Troops
Age: 39
Height: 5'9"
Birthplace: Albany, New York
Occupation: Carpenter

Pvt. William J. Sutphen
31st U. S. Colored Troops
Age: 18
Height: 5'3"
Birthplace: Rome, New York
Occupation: Boatman

The Sutphen family was the only colored family in Oneida County to enlist a father and son together. James Sutphen, also borne as Sutphin or Suthon, enlisted on December 19, 1863, in his hometown of Western. His oldest son, William, also known as Jerome, signed up with him that same day. Both men enlisted in the 16th New York Heavy Artillery.

From Utica the duo served as "sub-cooks of African Descent" in the artillery regiment. The original New York muster rolls list the pair as servants. Existing records show that the Sutphens served only about four months with the 16th N. Y. H. A. The Adjutant General's report, of that time, listed them as deserting from the camp at Elmira. But what in fact happened, was that the Sutphens transferred to the 31st United States Colored Troops.

The Sutphens were transported to Willet's Point in New York Harbor, where they joined their new unit on April 29, 1864. For some unknown reason the pair refused to be mustered in. However, the following day, both men were mustered.

The 31st United States Colored Troops began active campaigning in May of 1864 in Virginia. Their regiment took part in guarding the supply trains of the Army of the Potomac during The Wilderness Campaign. From there, they took part in the battles around Cold Harbor, June 2 – 12, then the Siege at Petersburg and Richmond. They fought at the Crater near Petersburg, July 30, 1864; Weldon Railroad, August 18-21; Fort Sedgewick, September 28; Hatcher's Run, October 27-28; and during the Appomattox Campaign in the Spring of 1865. That final campaign included the Fall of Petersburg and the pursuit and surrender of Robert E. Lee's army.

From Virginia, the regiment was sent to Texas in June of 1865. There they patrolled the Rio Grande until their muster out November 7, 1865, at Brownsville, Texas. The regiment suffered about 175 casualties during their term of service.

James received a promotion to the rank of corporal on July 30, 1864. He retained this rank until his mustering out. On March 20, 1865, he was assigned detached duty at the headquarters of the 3rd Brigade, 2nd Division, 25th Army Corps. James remained at this post throughout the summer. On November 7, 1865, James Sutphen was mustered out of the United States service.

William Sutphen, the son of James, followed a similar path as his father. He never received promotion in rank, nor was he detached for any special assignments. Records show William was sick from April 19, 1865, until August of 1865 in the hospital at Fort Monroe, Virginia. He mustered out on November 7, 1865 at Brownsville, Texas. His final discharge took place on November 28, 1865.

Father and son returned to Western after their expiration of service. The two men had left behind a wife and mother Sophia, age 26. Her age seem to indicate a second marriage for James. Two other sons and a daughter had been left behind when the pair enlisted. They were William and George, ages 15 and 6 years old. The daughter, Francis, was 10 years old.

Nothing else is known of the Sutphen family after the war. Neither man ever applied, for a pension which is a vital link in tracing the Civil War soldiers' later life.

General James H. Ledlie, a native of Utica, New York, commanded the 1st Division, 9th Army Corps on July 30, 1864, at the Battle of the Crater during the Siege of Petersburg. The United States Colored Troops engaged in the battle fought well, but the assault turned into a disaster under Ledlie's supervision, or rather a lack thereof. *(Author's Collection)*

UNITED STATES NAVY

Seaman Arlington Denike
United States Navy
Age: 23
Height: 5'5 ½"
Birthplace: Onondaga County, New York
Occupation: Barber

Utica barber, Arlington Denike left his wife Vilena at home in February of 1865 to join the United States Navy in New York City. Signing up on February 4, 1865, Denike started his naval life of four years on board the *U. S. S. Vermont.*

From the *Vermont*, he was transferred to the gunboat, *Preston*, which saw extensive service in the coastal waters of Virginia and the Carolinas. The *Preston* was deactivated at the end of July 1865 and part of her crew was assigned to the *Princeton*. Denike never reported to his new assignment and was listed as a deserter on August 9, 1865. During his service, he attained the rank of 1st class petty officer—a high rank for a man of color at this time.

Denike resumed his life in Utica after the war until the late 1890's when he moved to Auburn. From 1890 through 1905, he applied consistently for a pension, suffering from rheumatism, diarrhea and heart problems, but because of his desertion, Federal law denied Denike this benefit. Denike returned to Utica at the turn of the century. His death date is unknown.

Seaman William Henry
United States Navy
Age: 32
Height: 5'11 ½"
Birthplace: Prescott, Ontario, Canada
Occupation: Cook

Henry was one of Utica's most prominent colored citizens, and perhaps one of the oldest colored men to tender his services from Oneida County during the war. In 1865, Henry tried to enlist in Rhode Island in the Navy, but enlistments were not being accepted at this time. He then tried the Army, but was turned away because of being overweight. Henry traveled to Brooklyn where he successfully joined and was sent to the training ship *Vermont*. Later, Henry served as a landsmen on board the *Lady Sterling*, the *Hornet*, and his last ship was the *Princeton*.

While serving on the *Hornet*, Seaman Henry was stationed below Washington, DC, on guard duty the day that Mrs. Surratt and the rest of the Lincoln conspirators were hung. Henry stated that he could see her body swinging on the scaffold. The *Hornet* claimed to be the first Union gunboat to pass up the James River to the fallen city of Richmond. From the *Hornet*, Henry was transferred to the *Princeton*, but never reported. He deserted on January 13, 1866.

Before the war, Henry worked at numerous jobs at Addington's Pottery Works and on the Erie Canal. In his prime, he was 6' tall and weighed 397 pounds. Local lore states that he could lift 1700 pound hogsheads of tobacco to be placed on stands at his employer's Mooney & Howe's warehouse. Another legend states that he could slap a man unconscious because of his great strength.

Henry returned to Utica after the War and once again worked numerous jobs until hindered by rheumatism. During this time Henry was also a well-known figure for serving in several city fire departments. It is not known when he passed away, but he was 93 when the *Saturday Globe* did an article on him in 1904.

Seaman William Henry was one of Utica's most colorful citizens. Henry was portrayed here as a young man on one of his many jobs. The sketch appeared in the *Utica Saturday Globe* on July 30, 1904.

WILLIAM HENRY.

Seaman William Henry. In this view, Henry is shown as an elderly citizen relaxing. Both photos came from an interview that was carried by the *Utica Saturday Globe* on July 30, 1904.

Seaman George W. Johnson
United States Navy
Age: 32
Height: 5'10"
Birthplace: Delaware County, New York
Occupation: Cook

Johnson left Utica in December of 1863 to enlist in the United States Navy. On December 11, 1863, he signed up at the Boston Naval Yard for duty on the *U. S. S. Niphon* for a period of one year. During his term of service he also served a short stint on board the *U. S. S. Ohio*. While aboard the *Niphon*, Johnson lost a middle finger on his right hand and the use of two other fingers. While the *Niphon* cruised the southeastern coast, Landsmen Johnson participated in the naval attack upon Masonboro Inlet, North Carolina, on August 24, 1864, and the pursuit of the famed Confederate ship *C. S. S. Tallahassee* on August 25, 1864. The vessel also did blockade duty in the South Atlantic coastal area.

Discharged on December 7, 1864, Johnson returned to his wife, Mary, in Utica. Some time after the war the family moved to Chicago, Illinois, where he worked as a laborer at various jobs. On March 13, 1874, Mary passed away. Fourteen months later, Johnson remarried, this time, to Jane Jackson of Chicago on May 12, 1875, by Justice of the Peace, Daniel Scully.

At the time of his death, Johnson was working as a watchman at the Great Northern Hotel in Chicago. The attending physician stated that his death was due to "injuries received by being crushed by elevator" on July 16, 1898.

Mrs. Johnson outlived George by 19 years, passing away on June 9, 1917, at their Dearborn Street home in Chicago. The Johnson's did not have any children.

Seaman John E. Lippins
United States Navy
Age: 20
Height: Unknown
Birthplace: Oneida County, New York
Occupation: Barber

Landsman Lippins was the first Oneida County colored citizen to enlist during the Civil War. The Navy was Lippins' choice, and he served for over three years. In a handwritten letter to W. S. Schley, Chief, Bureau of Recruiting and Equipment, on April 17, 1889, the veteran told his own service record. The letter read as follows:

Dear Sir,

I want to find out on authority, whether or not I am entitled to a bounty of $100.00 as promised me by Recruiting Officer Brown on my enlistment at #Cherry Street, New York City, on November 4th, 1861, as landsman on the U. S. ship *Santaigo de Cuba*. This was, he said, a government offer, and was read to me from the shipping articles, of which I have requested a copy from your department. I remained on the *Santiago de Cuba*, until December 1863, when I was transferred to the receiving ship *Ohio* at Charleston Navy Yard from which I was transferred to the monitor *Canonicus* in April 1864 and discharged on the James River November 3rd, 1864.

Respectfully,
John E. Lippins
757 W. Lake St.
Chicago

A statement from the Navy Department on October 15, 1910, substantiates this letter. The Naval Department's response also acknowledges that Lippins deserted January 30, 1864 and was apprehended February 17, 1864. He then finished out his enlistment honorably. Lippins served his time primarily doing blockade duty along the Atlantic Coast off the states of Virginia, and North and South Carolina.

With his military service completed, Lippins returned to Utica. Here, the City Directories listed him as a barber.

Lippins was married twice. His first wife was Mary Hill of Newport, New York. From this marriage, one son named William was born on November 19, 1867. Mary Hill Lippins died on December 27, 1876. Lippins then married again, to Ida Jackson on March 28, 1878, at Syracuse, New York. The Lippins lived in Syracuse, Utica, and Richfield Springs until 1882. While living in Richfield Springs, Lippins became a member of the Weldon Grand Army of the Republic Post 256. How long he was a member is not known.

From Richfield Springs, the family moved to Illinois where he worked as a singer, barber, and a porter. Ida Lippins was an entertainer by profession, causing intervals of separation in the marriage. From this union, two sons, Max and Byron, were born.

Later in life, Lippins developed a drinking problem that worsened as the years went by. Around 1896, Ida left John because of this. She had stated that he failed to financially support her which forced her to work. "He was never abusive," she stated, "just unwilling to support the family." They were never divorced.

Lippins was in and out of the Soldiers Home in Quincy, Illinois, and finally entered the Soldiers & Sailors Home at Bath, New York, in 1910. In 1904, Lippins had applied for a pension suffering from rheumatism, heart failure, and failing eyesight. He was granted a pension of $12.00 a month. After living only three months at the home, Lippins died of "Decubitus," at 9:40 a.m., July 24, 1910. He was 86 years old. Upon learning of her husband's death, Ida tried to collect a widow's pension. For some reason, John Lippins stated at his deathbed that he was a widower. This created serious problems for his second wife in obtaining her benefits. It is not known if she ever collected pension benefits or when she died. Her last known address was in Rochester, New York, in 1911.

Seaman Frederick Wells
United States Navy
Age: 19
Height: 5′5 ½″
Birthplace: Oneida County, New York
Occupation: Steward

Frederick Wells was the second Wells brother to leave his home in Utica to serve his country. Frederick, the younger brother, did not enlist in the Navy until February 6, 1865, at New York City.

The *Vermont* was the first ship Wells served on and was then transferred to the *Preston*. The *Preston* was a gunboat that was posted in North Carolina and the Virginia waterways. Government records show that Wells failed to report for duty to his next ship the *Princeton*. In August of 1865, he was recorded as a deserter because of his failure to finish his three-year contract with the navy.

Nothing is known about Wells after the war until the early 1900's when he shows up in Brooklyn where, presumably, he died. His wife, Rittie, tried to have his name cleared in 1910 so that she could collect his pension benefits. She failed and Mrs. Wells thus faded from local history records.

UNKNOWN REGIMENTS

Private Charles L. Baker
Regiment Unknown
Age: 21
Height: Unknown
Birthplace: Oneida County, New York
Occupation: Farmer

Baker has one of the most intriguing service stints of all of the Counties' colored soldiers. According to available information, Baker enlisted in the 97th New York Volunteers for 3 years, which was an all white regiment. From that unit, he reportedly joined the 54th Massachusetts Volunteer Infantry and campaigned with that outfit until July of 1865. However, no record is found in any state or federal archives of his service. Most likely, Baker served with the 97th as an officer's servant.

Baker's family lived in the second Ward of Utica. Baker came from a large family of 11. The family consisted of his father Thomas, age 41; mother, age 38; brothers, Jacob age 15, Levi age 12, George age 9, and Edward age 1. His sisters were Latisia, age 20; Jenette, age 14; Harriet, age 11; and Louise, age 5.

Private Frederick Martin
Regiment Unknown
Age: 15
Height: Unknown
Birthplace: Oneida County, New York
Occupation: Laborer

Martin is one of Oneida County's mysterious colored soldiers. Not much is known of Martin, except for one line in the 1865 New York Census. Line 23 denotes him as a laborer who became a soldier. At the time of the enumerator's visit, young Martin was in the service.

When Martin left home, he left behind his mother Harriet, age 45, three sisters, and four brothers. His father, Edward, age 51, died of consumption October 10, 1864.

The family resided in the town of Kirkland during the war. There was one Frederick Martin that served in the 117th United States Colored Troops, but he was not the same man since this soldier hailed from the state of Kentucky.

Private Jesse Washington
Regiment Unknown
Age: 18
Height: Unknown
Birthplace: Maryland
Occupation: Farm Laborer and Servant

Jesse Washington is another little known colored soldier from Oneida County. This 18-year-old soldier was listed as a servant and laborer on the farm of Giles Smith in Deerfield, New York.

The New York State Census of 1865 is the sole mention of Washington in local history. At least five other Jesse Washingtons served during the Civil War in colored regiments. One served in a cavalry regiment, one in an artillery unit, and three served in other infantry organizations.

Private William Williams
Regiment Unknown
Age: 22
Height: Unknown
Birthplace: West County, Tennessee
Occupation: Unknown

William Williams of Clinton was one of over a hundred William Williams who served in the United States Colored Troops during the Civil War. His Regiment is unknown and so is what he did during the war.

The Hinkley Grand Army of the Republic Post minutes of February 1921 notes "William Williams (a Colored) comrade was voted into the post." Another valuable find was Williams' obituary in the April 28, 1926, *Clinton Courier*. It reads as follows:

Death of William Williams

William Williams, (colored) a farmer and well-known Clintonian, died at his home in Utica April 21. He was born in West County, Tennessee in 1841, and served as a cook in the Union Army during the Civil War, being a pensioner at the time of his death. He came to Utica about 53 years ago, but for a number of years was a resident of Clinton, where he was employed during the summer months in "lawnin' it over," as he called it. Sometimes he did not have change when he was offered a bill in payment, but he found that a poor policy, so he said, "I carries change nuf now, so's I can bust a twenty dollah bill."

His wife died in 1918. He is survived by a stepson, Ira Williams of Utica. "Bill" Williams was a member of St. Paul's Baptist Church, Utica. The funeral was Friday and burial was made in Sunset Hill Cemetery.

Private James Wilson
Regiment Unknown
Age: 25
Weight: Unknown
Birthplace: Virginia
Occupation: Farmer

Having the common name of James Wilson, this soldier has a little known background. Only the smallest amount of information is available. Wilson was a farmer from the Town of Western who enlisted October 3, 1863. His regiment will probably never be known and his military exploits never learned.

Wilson had a small family at this time. His wife Delia was 24 years old, and his daughter, Mary, age 10 months, were left in the town of Western while he was in the army.

Unidentified soldier with rifle. *(Courtesy of the United States Military History Institute, Leonard A. Walle Collection)*

General Daniel Butterfield as Colonel of the 12th New York Volunteers.
Butterfield advocated the use and training of colored soldiers during the war.
(See Appendix 3 pages 110-114) *(Author's Collection)*

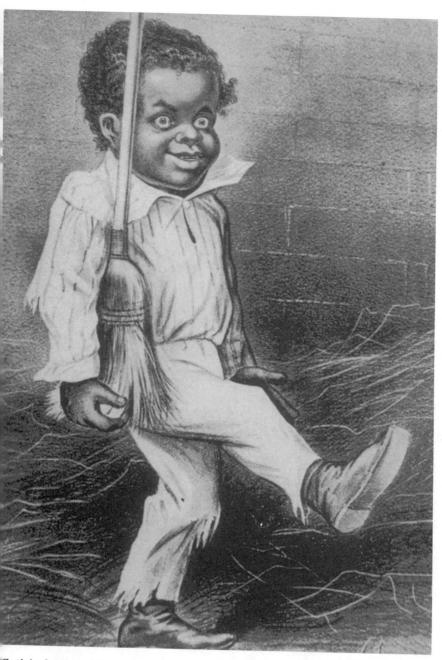

Satirical view of the colored recruit being trained. Brooms were sometimes used for training when weapons could not be procured. (*Author's Collection*)

The drawing of the draft in Utica, New York, in August of 1863. Amos Freeman and John Pell of the 4th Ward, Utica, had their names drawn at this time. Pell and Freeman's names, along with others, were published by the *Utica Morning Herald*, in an "Extra" on Friday, August 28, 1863. (*Courtesy of the Oneida*

Colored teamsters in winter quarters near City Point, Virginia. Private Norman Knox, 54th Massachusetts Volunteer Infantry, and Private James A. Williams, 29th Connecticut Volunteer Infantry, both were detached for teamster duty during the war. *(Author's Collection)*

Contrabands of War. From living conditions as this, Robert Wilson of Rome, New York, and Eli Bayliss of Utica, New York, escaped and served in the Union army. *(Author's Collection)*

View of Genesee Street, Utica, New York, looking north from Bleeker Street, circa 1854, from an ambrotype. Note bridge over the Erie Canal. Several colored soldiers from Utica worked in this area before the war. (*Courtesy of the Oneida County Historical Society*)

Post Street, Utica New York. circa 1880's. This was the residence of the Pell family who sent three sons off

(Courtesy of the Oneida County Historical Society)

Unidentified Civil War era colored woman. Most black women suffered immensely while their male family members were in the military. The dispute over equal pay caused many black soldiers not to accept it until the matter was resolved. This woman denotes a higher status in life by her hair style and stylish dress. The photo was taken in Penn Yan, New York. *(Author's Collection)*

Reunion of the 146th New York Volunteer Infantry on October 11, 1920, at the Courthouse in Rome, New York. Note the black veteran in the front row at the extreme right. At least six black veterans lived in Rome at the time

Grand Army of the Republic Decoration Day services at the First Baptist Church, Rome, New York, May 30, 1922. Note the two black veterans, in the first row 2nd from the right, and in the back center holding the colors. *(Author's Collection)*

A drawing by Alfred R. Waud showing United States Colored Troops after mustering out of service at Little Rock, Arkansas, circa April 20, 1866. (Library of Congress Collection)

Appendix 1

UNITED STATES COLORED TROOP OFFICERS
FROM ONEIDA COUNTY

1.	Gen. James H. Ledlie	Colored Division – 9th Army Corps	Utica
2.	Capt. William R. Brazie	1st & 5th United States Colored Troops	Utica
3.	Col. Benjamin Townsend	2nd United States Colored Troops	Trenton
4.	Maj. Milton B. Frisbie	3rd Louisiana Native Guard	Utica
5.	Capt. Robert T. Paine	5th United States Colored Heavy Artillery	Utica
6.	Lt. Williard W. Smith	6th United States Colored Troops	Rome
7.	Sgt. Robert Dryer *	7th United States Colored Troops	Utica
8.	Capt. Oliver Sturdevant	10th United States Colored Troops	Verona
9.	Lt. George E. Sutherland	13th United States Colored Troops	Utica
10.	Capt. George H. Foster	20th United States Colored Troops	Verona
11.	Lt. Col. Augustus G. Bennett	21st United States Colored Troops	Kirkland
12.	Lt. William Cornwell	21st United States Colored Troops	Annsville
13.	Chaplain Erasmus W. Jones	21st United States Colored Troops	Trenton
14.	Lt. George England	26th United States Colored Troops	Utica
15.	Lt. James E. Sprague	26th United States Colored Troops	Florence
16.	Lt. James H. Swertfager	26th United States Colored Troops	Waterville
17.	Lt. John H. Brown	27th United States Colored Troops	Trenton

18.	Lt. W. Lafayette Ames	38th United States Colored Troops	Stueben
19.	Lt. Richard Bascombe	38th United States Colored Troops	Rome
20.	Lt. Samuel B. Bancroft *	38th United States Colored Troops	Utica
21.	Lt. William E. Palmer	43rd United States Colored Troops	Utica
22.	Lt. Daniel Hitchcock	45th United States Colored Troops	Annsville
23.	Capt. William Knapp	76th United States Colored Troops	Bartlett - Westmoreland
24.	Col. Spencer H. Stafford	73rd United States Colored Troops	Utica
25.	Lt. Oscar W. Gulick	20th United States Colored Troops	Utica

* 7. White NCO used to train colored recruits.
* 20. Medal of Honor Recipient

Appendix 2

KNOWN BURIAL LOCATIONS

Pvt. William Anderson	Sterlingville, New York
Pvt. William H. Arch	Oakwood Cemetery, Chicago, Illinois
Pvt. William Avery	Rome Cemetery, Rome, New York
Pvt. Eli Baylis	Soldiers Memorial Site Forest Hill Cemetery, Utica, New York
Pvt. William J. Brown	Soldiers & Sailors Home Cemetery Bath, New York
Pvt. Henry Charles	Peterboro Cemetery, Peterboro, New York
Pvt. George W. Hall	Westernville, New York
Pvt. Cornelius Harding	New Forest Hill Cemetery Utica, New York
Sgt. Frances Henry	Soldiers & Sailors Home Cemetery Bath, New York
Pvt. Henry Howard	Old Burying Ground, Clinton, New York
Pvt. Wilbur Jackson	Fort Plain, New York (exact cemetery unknown)
Pvt. Foster Johnson	Rome Cemetery, Rome, New York
Pvt. Lewis Labiel	Cooper Street Cemetery Vernon, New York
Pvt. Charles W. H. Lloyd	Soldiers Memorial Site, Forest Hill Cemetery, Utica, New York
Pvt. Levi Palmer	Soldiers & Sailors Home Cemetery Quincy, Illinois
Sgt. John Pell	Camp Parapet Cemetery New Orleans, Louisiana
Pvt. Garrett S. Russell	Peterboro Cemetery, Peterboro, New York
Pvt. William J. Smith	Forest Hill Cemetery, Utica, New York
Pvt. William W. Smith	Rome Cemetery, Rome, New York
Pvt. Henry Simmons	Schaghticoke, New York
Pvt. Bradford Tompkins	Rome Cemetery, Rome, New York
Pvt. Peter Williams	Forest Hill Cemetery, Utica, New York
Corp. Samuel B. Williams	Soldiers Memorial Site, Forest Hill Cemetery, Utica, New York
Pvt. William Williams	Sunset Hill Cemetery, Clinton, New York
Pvt. Frank Wilson	Rome Cemetery, Rome, New York
Robert Wilson, Servant	Rome Cemetery, Rome, New York

A sketch done by Edwin Forbes near the Rappahannock River on the afternoon of May 6, 1863, entitled "Dick, the Company Cook."
(Library of Congress Collection)

A BIOGRAPHICAL
MEMORIAL *of* GENERAL
DANIEL BUTTERFIELD

INCLUDING MANY ADDRESSES
and MILITARY WRITINGS

Edited by

JULIA LORRILARD BUTTERFIELD

With Portraits and Illustrations

THE GRAFTON PRESS
NEW YORK   MCMIIII

GENERAL DANIEL BUTTERFIELD

While exertions are made, and with success, to raise regiments of colored troops, we find no general organization of a corps, that will give them the character and standing of white troops. In most instances they are scattered by regiments to perform the fatigue or garrison duty of armies in the field. Is this wise, as a matter of policy, disregarding all sympathies or antipathies toward these troops?

We are introducing a new element of great magnitude in the composition of our armies—one not at all unlikely, in case of future wars, to prove a great source of strength, as far as numbers are concerned. Is it wise, then, to ignore, in this element, its training and action in masses, on the march, in active campaign and in battle? Why should not the experiment be made of a column of these troops put in training at least? I believe that thirty thousand (30,000) colored troops, with proper condition, by necessary drill and discipline, will accomplish in ten days, marches, an average greater distance of five miles per day, with an average reduction of the transportation required, of fifteen per cent., by an equal number of white troops. I believe that I can accomplish this. How great an element of success such celerity of movement, with reduction of impedimenta, will prove, every soldier can appreciate.

The proper creation and fostering of this element of fighting strength in our country is worthy of the most careful consideration, both in a military and political point of view. Freedom is being extended to these people, many of whom are, in a great measure, unprepared by previous education and habits to take advantage of its benefits. Freed from the lash, and the fear of punishment, the surroundings of these people may cause indolence or crime to develop itself in such a manner as to cause many regrets for the political transformation of the race. The ordinary methods for the development of the untutored minds in civilized countries, would fail to meet the requirements of the sudden change in their condition. What better school, then, than that of the soldier for the men,

116

where the exercises and restraints of military rule and discipline will prevent the formation of vicious habits, and correct them, if already formed.

Not only a fearful responsibility, but a glorious work, is with the commanders of these troops. While performing all the duties required in a military point of view, it is absolutely necessary that a General-Commander of a large organization of colored troops should, if made, be possessed of enlarged views as to their political condition, their future uses in the State, and the necessities arising therefrom. A great power is placed in his hands for good, for evil, or, if a negative man, Providence and the future alone will shape the results. Without care, energy, comprehensiveness and ability, we must look forward to the probability of new troubles and difficulties arising from the discharge or expiration of service of these men— difficulties which may enter into the politics of the State, and, fed by the regrets of lost luxuries and ease, the bitterness and disappointments engendered by civil war, will aid in the creation of a political element that may override the stoutest efforts of the philanthropist or the progressive man. We may yet be thrown back a decade by such events as are here foreshadowed. How great, then, the necessity for prompt and prudent action in this matter.

Aside from the *esprit du corps,* which, with skill in arms, a commander will naturally inculcate, his efforts must not cease here. He must establish and effect a system of instruction in the plain elements of education, that will fix a basis at least for future development. His constant care and exertion will be required to improve their sanitary and physical condition. What a vast responsibility rests upon those who have allowed this class to die by scores, upon the Mississippi, during the last year, simply from a lack of personal attention and inquiry into their previous condition, mode of living, and the proper course to pursue with them.

The utility of these troops, the necessity for the increase of their numbers, that white labor may remain at the North, and slave labor be taken from our enemies, as well as for other reasons, are so generally admitted by every reasoning man, that any allusion to these points seems unnecessary. The commander whose vigilance should not be sufficient to keep his ranks full, where the material is so abundant within the scope of his operations, would fail to meet what is required of him.

The colored soldiers will draw periodically a certain amount of compensation from the Government. It will not matter what that may be, they will be left penniless at the expiration of their service, from harpies, sutlers and thieves, who will surround them, unless the commander shall organize and carry out a system of savings and investment for them, that will enable the soldier, should he so elect, at the expiration of his term of service, or at the close of the war, as the case may be, to purchase and stock, with the aid of his warrant, a freehold —become a cultivator of the soil for his own account—in other words, an independent man—a free citizen. Legislation will be required from time to time to aid in effecting these objects, and much labor, benevolence, firmness, energy and patriotism, from the commander, whose purpose, determination and objects becoming apparent, he will be fully seconded by his officers.

In a military point of view these organizations should be cultivated and improved to that extent, that they will be, with regard to the requirements of physical labor, entirely self-sustaining. The introduction of the various trades necessary to a complete organization of the corps should be made at once —by instruction where needed. A system of extending this instruction beyond the requirements of the regiment or corps will add much to the development of faculties in the black man, who has so long been kept down, that we ought, at least, to throw this chance in his way for light and improvement. These men should be taught self-government as fast as their mental development will permit.

I could go on *ad libitum* in the expression of views. I have given sufficient to shadow forth my ideas on the subject. I have thown them together hastily, and forward them in accordance with the wish expressed, when we met at the Century Club. They are perhaps crude, but they require no logical or rhetorical dressing out to reach the mind of a philanthropist as keenly alive to the necessities arising from pending questions as John Day.

You will not forget the admonition with regard to those officers who seek positions with colored troops, either for a commission, or to save being mustered out of service. Don't trust the man who boasts of his sympathy for this race, if he has any political aspirations, nor unless he knows and appreciates thoroughly what he talks about.

I have portrayed in feeble outline what might be done. It is a task of no trifling magnitude, and one from which I could almost shrink in contemplating the labor and devotion required—the trouble, difficulties and crosses to be encountered—did I not feel that the consciousness of having succeeded in such a task would be a far greater recompense to me than a hundred victories. Yet these may follow in the train.

The soldierly pride of these men must be aroused; their dress should be more brilliant; their *esprit du corps* strong. These efforts are never lost upon whites, even of our own race. Why should we ignore them with blacks? Napoleon's success with his Zouaves, Spahis, Chasseurs, etc., organized from the natives of Algeria, has its force as an example.

Accept this as it is written, without criticism upon any other point than its earnestness, the necessities involved, and its outline for meeting them.

DANIEL BUTTERFIELD, Major-General.

The word "State" used above is in its collective sense, as representing the country.

**"Going to the commissary for government rations. Culpeper Court House, Virginia, September 25, 1863."
Drawing by Edwin Forbes.** *(Library of Congress Collection)*

BIBLIOGRAPHY

Books

Adams,Virginia M., *On the Altar of Freedom*. University of Massachusetts Press, Amherst, Massachusetts, 1991.

Addeman, J. M., *Reminiscences of Two Years With the Colored Troops*. N. Bangs Williams & Co., Providence, Rhode Island, 1880.

Burchard, Peter, *Glory – One Gallant Rush*. St. Martin's Press, New York, New York, 1865.

Butterfield, Julia L., *A Biographical Memorial of General Daniel Butterfield*, The Grafton Press, New York, New York, 1904.

Cheney, W. H., *The Fourteenth Regiment Rhode Island Heavy (Colored)*. Negro Universities Press, New York, New York, 1898.

Durant, Samuel, *History of Oneida County*. Everts & Fariss, Philadelphia, Lippincott, 1878.

Dyer, Frederick H., *Compendium of the War of the Rebellion*. Thomas Yoseloff Publisher, New York, New York & London, 1976.

Emilio, Luis F., *A Brave Black Regiment – History of the Fifty Fourth Regiment of Massachusetts Volunteer Infantry 1863-1865*. Arno Press & The New York Times, New York, New York, Reprint 1891.

Fox, William F., *Regimental Losses in the American Civil War 1861-1865*. Albany Publishing Co., Albany, New York, 1893.

French, J. H., *Gazetteer of the State of New York*. Heart of the Lakes Publishing Interlahem, New York 1986.

Gladstone, William A., *Men of Color*. Thomas Publications, Gettysburg, Pennsylvania, 1993.

Main, Ed, *History of the 3rd United States Colored Cavalry*. The Globe Printing Co. and Reprint by Negro Universities Press, Louisville, Kentucky, 1908.

Montgomery, Horace, *A Union Officer's Recollections of the Negro as a Soldier*. Pennsylvania Historical Association, Harrisburg, Pennsylvania, Reprint 1961.

Newton, A. H., *Out of the Briars – Sketch of the Twenty Ninth Regiment Connecticut Volunteers.* Mnemosyne Publishing Co., Inc., Miami, Florida, Reprint 1969 of 1910.

Phisterer, Frederich, *New York in the War of the Rebellion.* J. B. Lyon & Co. State Printers, Albany, New York, 1912.

Redkey, Edwin S., *A Grand Army of Black Men.* Cambridge University Press, New York, New York, 1992.

Trudeau, N. A., *Voices of the 55th – Letters from the 55th Massachusetts Volunteers 1861-1865.* Morningside House, Inc., Dayton, Ohio, 1996.

Census Records

New York State Census of 1855 and 1865.

National Census of 1860 and 1870.

Institutions

National Archives – Military and Pension Records, Washington, D.C.

Clinton Historical Society, New York.

Oneida County Historical Society, Utica, New York.

Rome Historical Society, Rome, New York.

Utica Public Library, Utica, New York.

Newspapers

Utica Daily Observer, 1861 – 1865. Utica Public Library.

Utica Morning Herald, 1861 – 1865. Utica Public Library.

Utica Saturday Globe, 1882 – 1918. Utica Public Library and Oneida County Historical Society.

INDEX

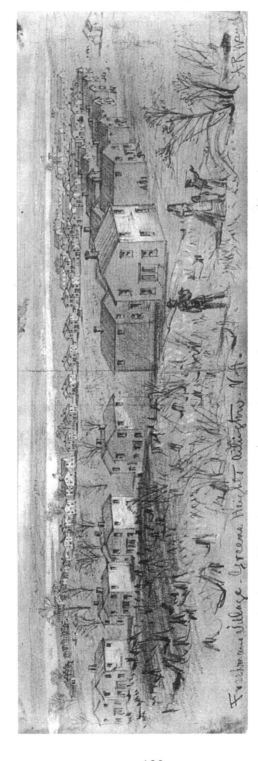

"Freedman's Village, Green Heights, Arlington, VA," sketched by Alfred R. Waud in the Spring of 1864.
(Library of Congress Collection)

For a complete book and price list write:

SCHROEDER PUBLICATIONS
131 Tanglewood Drive, Lynchburg, VA 24502
www.civilwar-books.com
Email: civilwarbooks@yahoo.com

Titles Available:

* **The Pennsylvania Bucktails: A Photographic Album of the 42nd, 149th & 150th Pennsylvania Regiments** by Patrick A. Schroeder ISBN 1-889246-14-X

* **Thirty Myths About Lee's Surrender** by Patrick A. Schroeder
ISBN 1-889246-05-0

* **More Myths About Lee's Surrender** by Patrick A. Schroeder
ISBN 1-889246-01-8

* **The Confederate Cemetery at Appomattox** by Patrick A. Schroeder
ISBN 1-889246-11-5

* **Recollections & Reminiscences of Old Appomattox and Its People**
by George T. Peers ISBN 1-889246-12-3

* **Tar Heels: Five Points in the Record of North Carolina in the Great War of 1861-5**
by the Committee appointed by the North Carolina Literary and Historical Society
ISBN 1-889246-02-6 (Soft cover) ISBN 1-889246-15-8 (Hard cover)

* **The Fighting Quakers** by A. J. H. Duganne ISBN 1-889246-03-4

* **A Duryée Zouave** by Thomas P. Southwick ISBN 1-56190-086-9 (Soft cover)
ISBN 1-889246-24-7 (Hard Cover)

* **Civil War Soldier Life: In Camp and Battle** by George F. Williams
ISBN 1-889246-04-2

* **We Came To Fight: The History of the 5th New York Veteran Volunteer Infantry, Duryée's Zouaves, (1863-1865)** by Patrick A. Schroeder ISBN 1-889246-07-7

* **A Swedish Officer in the American Civil War: The Diary of Axel Leatz of the 5th New York Veteran Volunteer Infantry, Duryée's Zouaves, (1863-1865)**
edited by Patrick A. Schroeder ISBN 1-889246-06-9

* **Campaigns of the 146th Regiment New York State Volunteers**
by Mary Genevie Green Brainard ISBN 1-889246-08-5

* **The Highest Praise of Gallantry: Memorials of David T. & James E. Jenkins**
by A. Pierson Case and New Material by Patrick Schroeder ISBN 1-889246-17-4

* **Where Duty Called them: The Story of the Samuel Babcock Family of Homer, New York, in the Civil War** ISBN1-889246-49-2

* **The Bloody 85th: The Letters of Milton McJunkin, A Western Pennsylvania Soldier in the Civil War** edited by Richard A. Sauers, Ronn Palm, and Patrick A. Schroeder ISBN 1-889246-13-1 (Soft cover) ISBN 1-889246-16-6 (Hard cover)

* **So, You Want To Be A Soldier? How To Get Started In Civil War Re-enacting** by Shaun C. Grenan, and edited by Patrick A. Schroeder.& Maria Dorsett Schroeder
ISBN 1889246-19-0

~~~~~~~~~~~~~~~~~~~~~~

Announcing the *Letters Home Series* by Schroeder Publications

This series will feature letters written home by Federal soldiers of famous regiments and brigades, as well as representative letters to family members from me of Union regiments of every state. These are poignant, descriptive, and historically informative letters to loved ones.

Letters Home: Letters to Mother ISBN: 1-889246-25-5

Letters Home: Soldiers of the 20th Maine Infantry ISBN: 1-889226-26-3

Letters Home: The Bucktails (Pennsylvania's 42nd, 149th, and 150th Regiments) ISBN: 1-889246-27-1

Letters Home: The Irish Brigade ISBN: 1-889246-28-X

Letters Home: The Iron Brigade ISBN: 1-889246-29-8

Letters Home: The Zouave Brigade (the 140th, 146th, & 5th Veteran New York Infantry Regiments and the 155th Pennsylvania Infantry) ISBN: 1-889246-30-1

Letters Home: Letters to Father ISBN: 1-889246-32-8

Letters Home: The Michigan Cavalry Brigade ISBN: 1-889246-33-6

Letters Home: The Vermont Brigades (Stannard's and the 6th Corps) ISBN: 1-889246-34-4

Letters Home: The Philadelphia Brigade ISBN: 1-889246-35-2

Letters Home: The Harvard Regiments (the 2nd and 20th Massachusetts) ISBN: 1-889246-36-0

Letters Home: Letters to Family and Friends ISBN: 1-889246-37-9

Letters Home: Letters of Battle ISBN: 1-889246-38-7

This series will provide a new, revealing, and richly informative material on the experience of the Civil War fighting men. Most books will be approximately 200 pages. Each book will contain numerous photographs, be printed in hard cover, with high quality acid-free paper, and have a foreword written by Historian Brian C. Pohanka. Each volume will cost approximately $24.95 (depending on size). Subscribe to the series and receive free shipping. Subscribe now at www.civilwar-books.com or email civilwarbooks@yahoo.com or call 888-888-1865.